I dedicate this book to every person who has ever felt lost, who has looked for support and mentorship in order to help them navigate through challenging seasons of their life.

I hope this book brings light and clarity to the dark and chaotic fragments of your life. My desire is that you gain the ability to dream again and then to make those dreams your reality!

James Beckford

I Can Fly in My Dreams: Conception to Manifestation

AUSTIN MACAULEY PUBLISHERS™
LONDON * CAMBRIDGE * NEW YORK * SHARJAH

Copyright © James Beckford 2024

The right of James Beckford to be identified as author of this work has been asserted by the author in accordance with sections 77 and 78 of the Copyright, Designs and Patents Act 1988.

All rights reserved. No part of this publication may be reproduced, stored in a retrieval system or transmitted in any form or by any means, electronic, mechanical, photocopying, recording or otherwise, without the prior permission of the publishers.

Any person who commits any unauthorised act in relation to this publication may be liable to criminal prosecution and civil claims for damages.

All of the events in this memoir are true to the best of the author's memory. The views expressed in this memoir are solely those of the author.

A CIP catalogue record for this title is available from the British Library.

ISBN 9781398495821 (Paperback)
ISBN 9781398495838 (ePub e-book)

www.austinmacauley.com

First Published 2024
Austin Macauley Publishers Ltd®
1 Canada Square
Canary Wharf
London
E14 5AA

I firstly want to thank God for his grace and mercy throughout my life; without Him none of this would be possible.

Next, I want to thank my wife, Coreene, for being at my side during this whole process and for helping me to create the space and time to finish this book. Thank you for your sacrifice and understanding.

I'd like to thank my mother, Audrey, for always believing in me and telling me what I was capable of—years before I saw it in myself. I've finally done it now!

I want to thank my dad, Calvin, for everything that he instilled in me from a young age that has helped me become the person I am today. I'm grateful for the discipline.

I can't forget my family who have been instrumental throughout my life, it truly takes a village!

Last, but certainly not least, a huge thank you to my mentors, Bishop Melvin Brooks and Dr Karl George. Thanks for challenging me and walking with me during this project, and for your words of counsel and support.

Table of Contents

Foreword	9
Preface	11
Chapter 1: My Genesis	13
Chapter 2: Earliest Childhood memories	18
Chapter 3: The LCI (Life Changing Incident) That I Needed	25
Chapter 4: When Real Life Kicks In	33
Chapter 5: Purpose – Revealed, Received, But Not Registered	47
Chapter 6: Show Me Your Friends and I'll tell You Who You Are	54
Chapter 7: Transitions	60
Chapter 8: From Religion to Relationship	71
Chapter 9: My Worst LCI… But '… It's Not Like Anyone Died'	76
Chapter 10: Life After Death	85
Chapter 11: Purpose Registered…?	95
Chapter 12: How Did You Get Here? Nobody's Supposed to Be Here	103
Chapter 13: The New Normal	109
Chapter 14: Character Development	116
Chapter 15: Character Development Part Two	126
Chapter 16: The Circle of Life	133
Chapter 17: Will You Be My Wifey? Say You'll Be My Wifey	142
Chapter 18: Engagement Ring to the Wedding Ring	151

Chapter 19: Two Become One	**160**
Chapter 20: Happy Wife, Happy Life	**167**
Chapter 21: Unprecedented Times	**173**
Chapter 22: New Seasons	**181**
Chapter 23: Conclusions and Life Lessons	**193**

Foreword

God has placed desires and dreams in our hearts to accomplish; however, many of us are afraid to dream big for fear of being disappointed. Instead, we look at others living incredible lives and think "that's not for me," and miss the doors God opens, which would lead us to happy and fulfilled lives. Jeremiah 29:11 reminds us that God has plans for us to prosper and not to harm us, plans to give us hope and a future. God wants good things for us, and we can't be afraid of dreaming BIG because God doesn't ever dream small, and He doesn't want us to, either. Once a believer understands that God has so much more for their life and understands that with GOD, anything is possible, the believer becomes UNSTOPPABLE!

James Beckford is an unstoppable young man. The Lord allowed our paths to cross a few years back, and upon meeting him, I knew that God was molding his life for the greater. The Holy Spirit led me to drop a few spiritual nuggets in his life, which challenged him and his plans for his life. A few years passed, and I looked up one Sunday morning, James was seated in our assembly. Not long after, James became a member of our church, and I became his Pastor and spiritual leader. Witnessing God working in this young man's life has been a joy. James is not only a faithful member of our church but a committed Christian who is studious and loves the word of God. His tremendous gift of teaching and preaching is a blessing to New J and the entire body of Christ. His loyalty and integrity are paramount in his everyday living. James and his wife, Coreene, are truly amazing, gifted people.

Today, you, too, can become UNSTOPPABLE and create YOUR version of an incredible life! Genesis 11:6 reminds us, "Nothing you have imagined you can do will be impossible for you." In other words, if you will dare to take God at His Word, you can manifest your dreams. Dream manifestation will be as big or as small as you want; it depends on how much work you are willing to do. There is no quick gimmick to manifesting your dreams and desires quickly.

However, you can begin the manifestation process with the roadmap you're holding in your hands, *I Can Fly In My Dreams: Conception to Manifestation* by my son in the ministry, Minister James Beckford. This book is a must-read! Manifesting the desires of your heart, goals, and dreams is essential to TRANSFORMING your life and fulfilling your God-divine purpose. Don't be afraid to fly in your dreams, for dreamers are the people who can change the world.

Bishop Dr. Melvin Brooks,
New Jerusalem Community Church, Sr. Pastor
Jabula New Life Ministries International, Deputy Presiding Bishop.

Preface

I am one of those people who have lucid dreams, for those of you who don't know what that means; it's when you're dreaming in your sleep, and you are aware that you are in fact dreaming and that it's not real. Much like a playing a video game, because it's not real, you can be as adventurous as you like and try things that you would never dare try in real life.

Growing up, like most young boys, I loved watching superhero films, one of my favourites was Superman. At that time, it was Christopher Reeves who played Superman. I would get a towel and a safety pin and wear the towel as a cape. Although I was relatively young and impressionable, I was very aware as to what was real and what was fake; so I would never jump out of the upstairs window and try to fly of course.

As I got older, whenever I was in a good place in my life and mind i.e. not in a place of fear, anxiety, low self-esteem etc. When I would have a lucid dream, I would just jump in the air and fly. I would imagine and visualise places and fly to them. However, whenever I was in a bad place, when I would have a lucid dream, even though I knew it wasn't real and that I could literally create my own reality, I would jump, but not be able to fly. I have found in my life, if I can't fly or imagine something in my dreams, then I certainly could never manifest it in real life. So, if you can't even conceive the thought, let alone imagine or dream about being happy, getting married, getting that job, that car or whatever your goals are. If you can't even imagine in your mind, if you can't even visualise it, if you can't fly in your dreams, then you won't fly in real life. Now of course I am using flying as a metaphor, but the principle remains.

In my life, there are a few things that I learned to do literally in my dreams, I would dream about certain activities, then I would learn and perfect the technique in my dreams before I ever tried it in real life, then when I tried it in real life, I was successful at them.

"Whatever your mind can conceive and believe, it can achieve."

I was asked a question at the start when I finally decided to write this book, the question was "why are you doing this?" I decided to write this book to tell my life story so far, with the intention of being as open and transparent as possible in terms of all my highs and lows and most importantly to show the lessons that I have learned.

I remember being at home some years ago during the winter season, there was fresh snow that fell overnight, and it was quite high and thick. The distance from my front door to the foot path was about 20 metres, as I made this short journey, I had to plunge deep into the freshly fallen snow with each step. By the time I got to the public foot path, the snow had gotten into my trainers and made the bottom of my trousers wet. Needless to say, I was far from impressed. However, as I reached the public foot path, there were numerous footprints in the ground from people who had previously walked the path. Now, instead of creating my own new footprints and getting wet, I could simply walk in the same steps of the previous walkers as they had created a path for everyone else – no discomfort was necessary. In the same way, with this book, I want to create a path through life for people reading this, so they don't have to rely on trial and error in areas of their lives.

Lastly, another reason as to why I am writing this book is to leave behind a legacy. When it's all said and done, one day I will no longer be here and it's the same for us all. I want something left behind, something that future generations, particularly my children, grandchildren and so on, can know and remember me by; with the ultimate intention of me inspiring and/or educating readers on key lessons in life. This is something that I personally wish that I had, some form of manual at the different stages in my life.

I'm grateful to God for my life and everything that I have been through so far, even the most difficult times; it's through the hard times that I have really grown and developed into the man I am today. Most of the best lessons that I learned in life have come through the worst and toughest situations in my life.

"We can't control what life throws at us, but we have a choice in terms of how we respond… so decide wisely!"

Chapter 1
My Genesis

The year is 1985 and we're in the month of September, David Bowie and Mick Jagger have the number 1 song in the charts 'Dancing in the Street'. The cost of The Times newspaper is just 25p and average house prices in the UK are circa £33.5K; what a time to be alive!

On the 2nd of September of that same year, my mother was in labour with me and was told late in the day that I was distressed in the womb and an emergency C-section would be needed. In the early hours of Tuesday 3rd September, I was born at 12:03am. What should have been a joyous moment for my parents quickly turned into moments of panic, despair, fear and uncertainty. I was still distressed and my heart stopped beating at three separate occasions, every second that my heart never gave a beat felt like an hour and each occasion where there was no beat felt like an eternity to my mother. As she lay helpless on the hospital bed, trying to read the doctor's facial expression to gauge what was happening; my mom whispered a short prayer, "Please God, don't make all of this be for nothing."

I imagine my mother having one of those moments where your whole life flashes before your eyes, before you arrive back in the present. Although I was never there, I can see her re-living her life nine months earlier in her mind, when she and my dad were just dating, with thoughts of getting married in the immediate future. My mom was 22 at the time, studying at Leicester university, whilst my dad was 20, also at university.

They arrived at this point by fate as some people would describe it. My dad and his sister Amelia had moved house, Lodge Road in West Bromwich, with my grandad; whilst their other siblings, Simon and Paula were raised separately by my grandmother. As my dad moved into Lodge Road, my grandad who was the primary provider had to work, leaving his children with a babysitter who was an elderly white woman – this was in the '70s. As time went on, my mom's grandmother, affectionately known as Mama noticed my grandad leaving home to go to work and leaving his children with the babysitter. Mama being Mama, a real nurturer began to start making extra food in her house to cater for my dad and aunty. She lived with my grandparents, Lloyd and Gloria Fletcher and their four children at that time: my mom, Polly the eldest, Mark and Sally. Their youngest daughter Abigail was still to come.

After she began making food for my dad and my aunty Amelia week by week, it naturally became a normal and regular occurrence for the Beckfords (my dad's side) to spend most of their time at the Fletcher's house, it was as if they were one family. Weeks turned into months, months turned into years and my parents grew up together as close-knit friends. As they got older, in their late teens/early twenties, their friendship that had developed in their childhood suddenly blossomed naturally into a romantic relationship.

My mother, as were the rest of her siblings, were known as "Mr Fletcher's children". This meant something to Mr Fletcher's children and to all those who knew them and the family. Being a Fletcher came with expectations and responsibilities, you couldn't do what you wanted or behave how you felt, as you were a reflection of Mr Fletcher. When my grandad Fletcher came over to the UK in the 1960s, he didn't just get a normal job like other most of his fellow immigrants. He became a magistrate, he always had leadership roles in jobs as if he was there to inspire other black men that they don't have to settle, but rather that the sky is the limit. He teamed up with my grandad Beckford and other leaders in the community who were also from an Afro-Caribbean origin, to set up organisations locally for the sole benefit of ethnic minorities. Mr Fletcher was well known and had a spotless reputation. Even when I was born and went to school and achieved good results, as the eldest grandchild, he would constantly remind me... "Well done, James, you're a Fletcher." This was something everyone in the family embraced from my oldest aunty down to the youngest grandchild at the time.

So after being raised in this royalty-like environment all her life, now at university getting ready to leave to get a job and start her life, my mother, Mr Fletcher's daughter now becomes pregnant outside of wedlock. Society back then, is nothing like how life is now. It was very rare for a couple to get divorced, back then, as it says in the vows, "It's until death do you part." Back then, it was a shame for a woman to get pregnant, never mind a Fletcher woman.

After informing my dad about my imminent arrival in five months, they decide to break the news to my grandad, Mr Fletcher. Notice I said break the news to my grandad not grandparents; my grandmother, Mrs Fletcher would be able to receive any type of news and maintain her composure. My grandad on the other hand… Well, this about 30 years before he gave his life to Christ, got baptised and began to produce the fruit of the Spirit.

My parents decided on a date to tell my mother's parents the news. My mother was sure to tell her siblings first and let them know which day to expect fireworks in the home. My aunty and uncle, just Teenagers at the time, responded by ensuring they would be out that evening and would only return home in the morning after the after math.

The day finally arrives, my parents come back home from their respective universities. They go to my grandparent's house to break the news. As stated earlier, my grandmother receives the news, though she is not happy about the situation, she keeps her composure and holds back on any comments. Now my grandad, Mr Fletcher… I wasn't there in AD 79 in Pompeii, when the volcano erupted and destroyed the area, but if you were looking for a human re-enactment of what happened; then my grandad's response to the news would have been very accurate. He slammed the living room door which is largely made up of glass, I'm told it's a miracle that it never shattered. He told my dad to get out of his house, before directing an onslaught of rhetorical questions at my mother; "is this what you've been studying at university?"

"What am I supposed to do now?"

"I'm going to have to move back to Jamaica, aren't I?"

It was the reaction that my parents were expecting but did not want or need. My mother went back to Leicester to finish university. A great deal of time went by and still not one word was exchanged between my mother and grandfather. Suddenly, my mom became really ill, which was the cause of my grandad reaching out to my parents.

My mom, now beginning to show in her belly, is now feeling the shame and embarrassment of getting pregnant before being married. There were no mobile phones, social media or any IT communications, but news travelled fast that Mr Fletcher's daughter was pregnant. My family had close ties to the local church, to the point that after services, people would just show up at my grandparent's house. Now that my mom was pregnant, every time there was a knock at the door, she would go upstairs and stay there until the guests had left. It was an eventful five months to say the least.

Now we're back in the hospital, after everything that my mom has been through in the last five months, having just gone through an emergency C-section, having endured embarrassment, shame, guilt, tarnished the family's name, had a breakdown in the relationship with her father, now the whole reason she went through this, me… is now clinically dead. Questions began to swim around in her head, "What was all this for?", "If this is it, it would have been better never to get pregnant in the first place, rather than go through this."

With her eyes fixed on the doctors, with her eyes saying, "Please, please give me good news." The doctor looks back at her and before they can verbalise a response, their body language and eyes let my mom know that it's okay Mrs Beckford, your baby is alive.

Throughout different stages of my life, I often wondered why I made it through as a baby, whereas many other babies didn't. Is there an element of divine intervention, either by God directly, or by the prayers of others? Or does God allow things to play out without getting involved?

I ask these questions from both vantage points, with the mind that different people, with different beliefs may read this. Now anyone that knows me, knows that I subscribe to the God factor, in other words, God is and was a huge factor in my story and my beginning. I believe that I am here on planet earth and I entered on 3rd September at 12:03am ON purpose, BY purpose, WITH purpose and FOR a purpose. My heart could have simply stopped and never gave a beat again and that would have been my entire life – a few minutes. But almost 40 years later, the same heart that wasn't able to function, continues to beat until now… and I am grateful to God.

I could have been born in the 1600s or at any other random time. But God would so have it that I would be born at time, that would mean I would be here at the conception of the internet and social media. When I was in high school, that was the era when people started getting mobile phones. I am living in a point in time where mankind's knowledge has skyrocketed in such a short space of time. A person can lay in their bed and reach the entire world from their phone. Anything that you want to know, in most cases can be found online. I say all that to say this, surely because I am here, there must be a reason, surely because I'm living in the twenty-first century, there must be a reason. This is what life is all about, finding your 'Why'?

> *"To everything there is a season, and a time to every purpose under heaven: a time to be born…"*
> *Ecclesiastes 3:1–2*

At my birth, I had my first LCI – Life Changing Incident. This is a term I first heard from one of my mentors, Dr Karl George. It's an event in your life that alters the trajectory of your life whether for good or for bad. As we move forward, I'll reveal my other LCIs.

Chapter Reflections

- *Why were you born and what is your purpose here on earth?*
- *Have you ever had a near death situation, if so, has this changed your perspective on life? If so, how?*
- *When you die, what do you want to be remembered for?*

Chapter 2
Earliest Childhood memories

"You don't know where you're going until you know where you've been."

My earliest childhood memories start when I was five years old. As the quote explains, it's important to know where you're coming from in order to effectively move forward in areas of your life and life in general. It's good to get to know yourself and this starts from your childhood and all things you experienced that contributed to make you who you are today.

For me, I felt that I had a good childhood, growing up in the early days in a two-parent home, with both parents working what society would call 'good jobs' and getting 'good money'.

My earliest childhood memory goes back to my 5th birthday party. It was held at my Grandparent's house, which everyone till this day calls 'Hill Top'. It was and is the headquarters for the family, there's been many family events and it's also been an open-door policy to the community.

At my fifth birthday party, all my family were there, I had my closest cousins there – Max and Charlotte. Both are from my dad's side of the family and were my only cousins at the time, that I really knew. Max, the oldest cousin was born just 11 days before me and Charlotte was a couple of years younger. We grew up very close to each other when I was young, spending a lot of time at each other's house, sleep overs and time at my other Nan's house – Nanny Beckford.

The highlight of my birthday was when I was told to close my eyes in anticipation for my main gift. As I opened my eyes, my dad wheeled in a red bike with stabilisers. As you can imagine, I was more than excited. I suppose that day summed up my earlier years – family and good times.

It was when I was five that my parents bought their first house in Willenhall, after moving from a flat in Handsworth Wood. I don't remember anything about the flat, but I remember moving into our house and the walls been stripped back to the bare walls until they got wallpapered. Although, we lived in Willenhall, 90% of my childhood and adult life would take place at my mom's parent's house – Hill Top. I didn't go to school in the area where we lived, I went to school by Hill Top. Every weekday, we woke up, my mom would drop me to Hill Top, then my Nan would take me and my aunty Abigail, who is a few years older than me, to school – we grew up like brother and sister. After school, my nan or grandad would pick us up from school and take us home (Hill Top). I was raised on my nan's cooking, after dinner I would do my homework with my grandparents and then play with Abigail. My mom would finish work and get back to my Hill Top around 7 pm every day, she would eat dinner from Hill Top, then we would watch TV soaps and go home. We literally only slept in our house.

On weekends, we would have breakfast at home on a Saturday, then we and all the family (my grandparent's children and grandchildren) would go to Hill Top for dinner – Saturday Soup. On Sundays, the whole family would go to church and then everyone again would go to Hill Top for dinner. Hill Top felt more like home than my actual home. I grew up like this from the age of five and this routine would remain for many decades.

From the age of 5, or even from when I could first speak, I always called my grandmother 'Mommy Fletcher' and my grandfather 'Daddy Fletcher', they were like parents to me and so instrumental in my life. A lot of the other grandchildren started out calling them Mommy and Daddy Fletcher but would change as they got older. I think I was the only one to always call them that.

Growing up, as you can tell, I spent all my time around my mom's side of the family and only a small amount around my dad's side. Right or wrong, this was the just the case.

When I started attending school, I was a very confident child, not shy. Both my grandads were huge advocates of education, especially with their experience as black men entering the UK in the 1960s. They taught their children, that as black people, we need to work twice as hard as everybody else and be twice as educated as everyone else to even be considered in the working world. This was passed down to my generation too.

In primary school, I excelled in most subjects, I remember being five years old and the only person in my class who knew how to tie shoelaces, so the teacher would send pupils to me for me to show them how to do it. This is something that came from my grandparents, that mentality of not just being like everyone else, but striving for excellence, or as Daddy Fletcher would say, being a 'Fletcher'.

The school that I went to was predominantly white school. I remember my first day in Year 1, there was only one other black boy in the whole school. Situations like this seriously impact on a child's identity and how they see themselves. That's why it's important, that although children go to school to learn certain subjects, there is a need for a parent to educate their children on topics that the education system does not have on their curriculum.

I remember it being time to draw yourself and your family; all the white kids picked up pink crayons to colour their skin, being the only black boy in the class, I didn't want to be the only one looking different. Besides at that age, I asked myself, "I am black, so do I use a black crayon or a brown crayon." So for a whole year, I coloured myself with a pink crayon to fit in with everybody else. At no point did my teacher say anything to me, looking back, it seemed like she was okay for me to reject and be Ashamed of who I was – a black boy. It took me another year, when I was in year 2, to finally get the courage and confidence to finally pick up the brown crayon, complete my picture and then hand it in to the teacher. I was finally able to fly in my own mind and be who I was created to be.

Because my school, was mainly a white school, it meant my first reference or my first attraction was to a white girl – now there's nothing wrong with this. My point is if you only have one option, you can only make one choice, you can only get what's there. I hate when I go to McDonalds and go to order a milkshake, then they tell me the machine isn't working, it means I have no choice but to pick whatever is left over.

When I was in year five in Junior school, one of the biggest girl bands was the Spice Girls. I remember all the boys would talk about how attractive they all were, but would never mention Mel B, the 'black one'. Again, things like this affect a child's perception and ultimately their decisions. If a black child is in a school with an even mix of races and they choose a white girl, then fair enough, that's THEIR choice. But when a black boy is raised in a white school, where a teacher makes him feel okay to be ashamed to be black and the other white boys (and it's their choice) put white girls on a pedestal, but put black girls down directly or indirectly, then that black boy's choice is skewed and his choices are psychologically picked for him. This impacts their decisions, high school, college, university and even to the point when they go to pick a wife.

"A child's identity, their 'whoness' and 'whatness' should come from home, not school, external sources or social media."

Looking back in my life, it seems a lot happened when I was five, or around that age. When I was five, I had my first LCI (Life Changing Incident) that I was conscious about. As mentioned, Abigail and I were raised like brother and sister and fought like cat and dog, like most young siblings. At that time, at Hill Top, after the front door where you walk in, there was a porch door. In those days, we had single glazed windows in the doors. So as Abigail and I engaged in our daily fight, I was by the porch door, Abigail pushed me and I fell back and went completely through the glass in the door. My Nan came running round to see what had happened. I was crying and Abigail was in shock. My nan sat me down on the chair in the dining area, next to the fridge. I still had my school shirt on. My adrenaline is running high, I don't even notice that my shirt on my left arm is slowly turning red. The glass had gone into my arm and there was a 'C' shape scar that covered my whole left forearm. The cut was so deep that my skin could fold back.

We rush to A&E, my mom meets us there. I had cut the top of my head, my arm and the back of my left leg. I had to get 19 stiches on my arm and about six on the back of my leg. I would be scared for the rest of my life and have that awkwardness forever where people stare at me with a look of disgust on their face and ask, "What happened to your arm?" Again, I'm five, so things like my personal image and self-esteem haven't come into the equation yet, but they would be waiting for me.

There are parts of that night that I don't remember. My mom tells me the story of how they had to put her outside the operating area whilst they put the stitches in. She remembers them drawing the curtain, whilst her five-year-old son cried and bawled for his mom, but there was nothing that she could do, as it was necessary pain. She explained to me, that as a parent there are times where you would rather swap places with your child and take the pain for them, rather than watch them suffer, especially when there is nothing you can do to take away their pain. This would be a feeling that I too would face one day.

My next LCI would take place in the same year, when I was five years old. This was another negative incident that would literally change who I was, from the inside out and also come with knock on effects that have affected me all my life.

At Hill Top, Mommy Fletcher and Daddy Fletcher decided to open their home and become foster carers, around the same time my nan's sister Helen did the same. My grandparents did this for almost three decades, taking on different young people, with different racial profiles and life experiences.

Being a foster carer isn't something that you do for the money, I'm not sure what it pays, but I know that money can't be your motivation, otherwise you won't last long. It's not a job where you work from 9–5 and then go home, switch off and have the weekend to yourself. It's a 24-hour job and you're dealing mostly with young people who have some form of behavioural issues as a result of their past experiences. This was certainly my observation growing up.

One day, some of the family were at Helen's house, I don't remember who was there, again, I'm five years old. All the adults were downstairs doing what adults do, this was my perspective at this young age. Helen at the time was fostering a young person, can't remember their name or much about them really. It was just us two upstairs in their room… even recalling this to put pen to paper is very difficult, having to dig into my past, to my earliest childhood memories and re-live the event Without going into any details, as it doesn't add any value, I was abused, sexually. It would be more than 15 years plus before I told anyone or even felt comfortable talking about it.

Just like when I was in hospital when my heart stopped beating three times and it looked like I would never breathe again, just as I questioned why I was kept alive vs many other babies that were in the same situation as me. I again questioned why this abuse happened to me at five years old. I have Godchildren and nieces around the same age and can't understand why anybody with sense and a conscience would want to harm an innocent child. This is a question that I pondered on all through my life. As a Christian who prays, there were many prayers that I prayed to try to get understanding. I think in life, when bad things happen, we all want to understand why it happened so we can rationalise the situation. I've learned in life that you won't always reach an answer whilst you're here on this earth. Sometimes life just happens, we live in a world where people aren't robots controlled by God, rather, people have a free will and can choose to make whatever decisions they like based on whatever motive they have. As I said earlier, in life we can't choose how life treats us, but we can choose how we respond.

This was not just a one-off abuse that happened and that was it. As I said, I changed from the inside out and this was something I noticed in myself at the time and more so now that I am older. My personality changed, before I was always confident and fearless, now this reservedness and shyness kicked in. I remember that change in myself at school from year 1 to year 2. It was like my soul was split and another version of me was created. At any given moment, I was my normal self, then in a split moment I would change my demeanour, outlook and whole character. This is something that I see in myself to this day, whilst at work, church or around people in general. I can be either extremely confident and okay, or extremely shy and reserved; I can either fly in my dreams or not be able to fly…

When I was abused, it opened my mind to a world that should be reserved for adulthood or at least puberty. I'm now five years old and have these feelings and desires. I'm now experiencing feelings of arousal, something that I have never known or felt before. I can't imagine my God children who are about the same age, feeling like this of even having a clue about any of this.

"Protect your children!
Physically: by being as aware as possible of their company – family or not!
Spiritually: pray for your children, because sometimes you will have no idea what they are going through."

Children's innocence needs to be protected and that's me speaking from experience. This is why, in my opinion, a child should NOT be taught sexual education before high school and they certainly should not be forced to choose their sexual preference and/or gender. Let them be children and don't rob them of their innocence and childhood.

So I'm just five years old and been through two LCIs, the scars after going through the glass door at Hill Top and now the abuse. The worst thing was that the consequences of both incidents wouldn't kick in until later in my life.

Chapter Reflections

- *Did you struggle with a part of your identity when you were young or are you even struggling now?*
- *Do you love who you are completely? If not, why?*

- *Do you have any resolved issues from your past that you have buried and never dealt with?*
- *Are there things in your life that you can't accept and come to terms with?*

Chapter 3
The LCI (Life Changing Incident) That I Needed

I am now 10 years old, it's now 1995, Mark Jordan has returned to the NBA, DVDs had just been created, ready to be released two years later. Toy Story the movie premiers, Bill Colin is president, OJ Simpson got set free and the Internet was privatised and took off.

I'm now in year 5 at my primary school – Hately Heath, just two years away from high school. Life is pretty good, the two negative LCIs are a distant memory whilst the consequences remained mostly dormant. Things were exactly the same from my earliest childhood memories; wake up at my house, get dropped to Hill Top, go school, go back to Hill Top and then home again – just how I liked it.

Before on a Sunday, I would go to church with my mom, whilst my dad did his own thing. Prior to my mom getting pregnant with me, they both went to church, however after the attention my mom received after getting pregnant, she vowed never to go to church again, but Dad remained. Somewhere in the first five years of my life things changed, and they completely switched roles.

On a Sunday, my dad would play Sunday league football, so I had a choice, I could either go to church with my mom or go football with my dad – obviously I chose football. At that age, church was boring, the singing was okay, but after that, it was just long and the preachers didn't know time management… in my 10-year-old mind.

This went on for some time, until one night I had a dream. Now you have to understand, at this point I knew there was a God and his name is Jesus, but that's all I knew. I had no concept of end time, apocalyptic Bible events. So, when I'm dreaming about the second coming, where I see a man who I identified as Jesus appearing in the sky as a frowning judge, with an angry look on his face, I was both shocked and petrified to say the least. In the dream, He speaks to me as everyone is on the floor bowing or lying prostate in both reverence and fear, great and small. I don't remember what He said, all I knew was as soon as He finished, I woke up in the middle of the night, ran into my parent's room and slept on the floor. I didn't want to be alone. This was the first of many dreams.

Not much time went by, then Abigail having her own conviction decided to get baptised. Not long after, with the assist of more dreams, I decided to get baptised, the date would be 3rd March 1996 at our church's headquarters – Gibson Road.

During the time between my first dream and my baptism, my knowledge and understanding hadn't increased that much. I just understood that there is a God, there is a heaven and hell and that I didn't want to that angry face again. Back in those days, in churches, there was a lot of preaching about heaven and hell, as a way to warn people, nowadays you don't really hear these types of messages, I guess people don't want to offend anyone or they would rather give a message that tells people what they want to hear.

A few days before the Sunday of my baptism, I get another dream. This time, I'm at Hill Top and I am walking down the stairs, as I turn left to go towards the kitchen, I am struck down to the floor by God. It's a dream, but it feels real at the time. It's an indescribable feeling, it's a new feeling. As I'm on the floor, Mommy Fletcher and Helen come round and are like spiritual midwives. I have seen people in church 'get in the Spirit' and then speak in another language and now in my dream, it's happening to me. Something inside me is speaking another language and at the same time with my own vocal chords I am speaking and saying the highest praise to God – Hallelujah. I'm receiving God's Spirit with evidence, just as it says in the Bible, but it's happening in my dream. So now I have this same expectation when I wake up ahead of my baptism.

We go to our church at Kelvin Way, West Bromwich on the morning of my baptism, back then there was always services on a Sunday, morning and evening service. It seemed like a normal service that morning, the usual Sunday school, choir marches in, scripture reading, prayer and the preaching. But when it was time for the altar call, where they call people to the front to be prayed for, this time, I would get a taster and the first instalment of the LCI that I needed.

My mom makes eye contact with me, she was on the choir so was at the top on the rostrum whilst I sat in the congregation. She signalled at me to come to the altar, so I went. I knelt down and my mom began to speak to me. She told me to give God the highest praise and say hallelujah, so I just obeyed. I began to say and repeat the word Hallelujah, after about 30 seconds, I begin to feel different – what is this feeling? Tears began to start and flow – why am I crying? I'm 10 years old with a very limited understanding of the Bible and God, but all I know is that I can feel something on the inside of me, an atmosphere is over me, almost like going into a steam room and instantly observing the change in the environment. My eyes are closed, and I partially am conscious that I am now standing, I can hear people around shouting, "Yes, yes, that's it, come on." I'm told that Helen was 'in the Spirit', she started sitting at the back of church, but she moved uncontrollably through all the chairs, going from row to row and now we are holding hands dancing. Now if you know me, I have two left feet and no rhythm, but now I am dancing... in rhythm. I thought what I had experienced was what they call been filled with the Holy Spirit, but when church finished, I was told it comes with the evidence of speaking in another language as described in the book of Acts, chapter 2.

I remember my uncle Gerald, my aunty Polly's husband, saying that I would definitely get 'filled' when I got baptized. Church finishes and the family all goes back to Hill Top, to eat and rest before we go to Gibson Road church in the evening so I can get baptized.

I recalled the dream that I had recently had of being filled, where the Holy Spirit was speaking through me in tongues/another language, whilst I simultaneously was saying Hallelujah. So naturally, this was my expectation of how I would get filled, I just needed to wait for the Holy Spirit to speak whilst I said hallelujah.

We go to Gibson Road that night, they have the normal service first, then baptisms at the end. It's now time, I get changed into my baptism clothes, my mom is with me with the changing bag in the changing room for moral support and to make sure I'm okay.

I walk into the pool, there's a crowd, as was normal whenever anyone got baptized. Back then different people would tell you about their experience of how they got filled, with the intention of encouraging and educating you. But the more people who spoke to you, the more confused you were in terms of what your experience would be.

My auntie Mia, Mark's wife, at the time got baptized not too long ago. As soon as she got baptized, when she was walking out the pool, she just began speaking in tongues, this was my expectation. I get baptized, plunged under the water and then lifted back out again... there's nothing. Where is that feeling that

I had at church at the altar, earlier that day? Where was the Holy Spirit to speak in tongues for me like in my dream? I didn't understand, this was very anti-climactic.

I get changed back into my clothes in the changing room. My mom said we will go back to the altar to pray just like we did in the morning. There's an altar worker with my mom, like spiritual midwives, just as I had experienced in my dreams. I am saying hallelujah just like I did in the morning… nothing. I start shouting and screaming hallelujah at the top of my voice. I thought the more energy that I gave, the more chance there was of me getting filled. After some time, we stop. I'm not filled. Why am I not filled? What have I done wrong?

We go home, my mom begins to educate me about fasting and the power that it has. She tells me to fast and pray to be filled. Over the next couple of days, I test out fasting. I was told to fast until midday as it was my first time. So I'm at Hill Top and I just chill out and watch TV until 11:55am, then I put food in the microwave for five minutes, so that as soon as the food is ready, the fast would be over – this fasting is easy!

My mom comes back from work and asks how the fasting went, I told her what I did and of course she had to explain that it's not just about not eating, it's about prayer, reading the bible and spending time in worship. I take on board everything she said and try again the next day.

On Wednesday, 6th March, three days after my baptism, we had midweek church service, in this season it's tarrying service, this is for people who aren't filled with the Holy Spirit to have the entire service to try.

I start by doing what I did on that Sunday morning, when I had that first encounter, giving the highest praise – hallelujah, things feel the same as they did that Sunday morning. In my mind, I am waiting for the Holy Spirit to speak for me like in my dreams, it must have been for at least 30 minutes. Then after some time, I don't know if this was placed in me by God, but I stopped waiting and moved in faith. I began to open my mouth and let the Holy Spirit lead me in terms of the words I would say. I didn't think about, try to understand it or rationalize it, just faith. I spoke in another language and everyone around me was ecstatic, shouting and praising God. I was filled with the Holy Spirit and my life would never be the same again, this was the life changing incident that I needed and things would only get better.

At first, I wanted to be filled so that if I was to die, I wouldn't go to hell or when Jesus comes back, I would have this 'passport' that would allow me to go to heaven. But this experience was just the tip of the iceberg.

"We have this treasure in this earthen vessel." 2 Corinthians 4:7

So now I am filled. My Pastor at the time says for me to go on the choir, that was made up of around 10 women in their 30s, including my mom and aunty. I didn't fit in with the other kids at church, but I also didn't fit in with people on the choir. I didn't have anyone like me around, just like when I started school and was the only black boy in my class.

I had a strong passion for God even at 10 years old, my mom would buy me books from Christian shops, that were designed for young people and made the Bible characters into a comic like book. My first two characters were Nehemiah and then Dean. I loved Dean, a young guy who had dreams, living in an imperfect environment, I could definitely relate with him.

My mom taught me how to read the Bible, back then, there wasn't all the different translations that we have now to make things easier, it was just the King James version, and I loved it and still do. My mom taught me how to read and how to pray and ask God for understanding of the Bible. Since then, I've always been able to get understanding, revelation and see things. This made reading and fasting very enjoyable, which was a strange thing to see back then and even today. I was definitely different and was always told by people around me.

Being baptised and filled was great, but it didn't mean life would be easy and smooth sailing. It did however mean that I had an anchor for the upcoming storms in my life and it did mean I would find peace in the darkest parts of my life.

The year before, when I was nine years old, my aunty Sally had converted to Islam, which was a big shock to the whole family, especially as most people where devout Christians. My aunty Sally, like a lot of people in my family went to church but didn't really know and understand the Bible. So when Sally met some Muslims who knew the Quran AND the Bible and could break down and explain scriptures from a Muslim perspective, it made sense for her to become a Muslim. From her perspective, these people know their religion and their God and can communicate their faith effectively. Sally was all in, learning Arabic, buying Islamic books and attending Mosque services.

I recall my mom confronting Sally and asking her what she was doing, but by the time Sally had finished speaking and breaking things down, my mom nor people in my family had answers. This was a huge wake up call to my entire family. Shortly after, Mommy Fletcher set up our family Monday night prayer meetings, that are still going to this day – almost three decades later!

> *"Then Jesus told his disciples a parable to show them that they should **always** pray and not give up." Luke 18:1 (NIV)*

Sally then got married and had her second daughter Shabeena, she was born whilst Sally was a Muslim, hence the name. In this season, I would learn and witness the power of prayer and fasting. For three years, I watched Mommy Fletcher lead her family in prayer to bring her daughter back into church. Meanwhile, Sally would come to Hill Top with full Islamic attire and bring her Quran everywhere with her. Mommy Fletcher would go to the front door where Sally's shoes were, if she had a handbag or any other items, Mommy Fletcher would get olive oil which represents the Holy Spirit and anoint Sally's stuff and intensely pray for Sally.

Three years later, in 1997, Sally has kept her word – never to step back into a church again. She missed my cousin Shane's christening, Mark and Mia's first born and also a friend's funeral to honour her word. There was an annual church meeting in Wolverhampton, All Saints church, the Pastor was Pastor Powell and the preacher was Dr Cawley from Canada. My mom invited Sally to come to church, despite Sally's vow and despite the fact that she missed two important events recently. For some reason, Sally agreed to go.

I remember this night. I was sitting next to Sally in church and I had a tape recorder to record the preaching. Dr Cawley was preaching and must have been close to or in the middle of his crescendo. As he is preaching, he shouts, "Budda is dead, Mohammed is dead, but Jesus is alive!" I don't know what happened to Sally, but just like me in my dream when I got filled, she was on the floor under the power of the Holy Spirit. I couldn't believe it at first, I had watched Sally be a Muslim for three years, even have a baby and give her a Muslim name, now here she is in church at the altar prostrate.

> *"At the name of Jesus, every knee should bow… and that every tongue should confess that Jesus Christ is Lord." Philippians 2:9*

It wasn't long before Sally was back at church, on the choir and then speaking in another language at choir practice. Prayer works, God is real and all things are possible!

This is in 1997 and I am now 11 years old about to turn 12. I remember at this age wanting a sibling, I had younger cousins on my mom's side that I see regularly at Hill Top, Rachel and Dean, who are four years younger than me. I also have Luke, Dean's brother, Shane and Shabeena, but they're toddlers at this point.

Fresh off the back of praying and interceding for Sally, my aunty Polly introduces me to cheques that are from 'The Bank of Heaven'. You just write down what you want on there, like a blank cheque and at the bottom right-hand corner, it has a signature that had been signed in Jesus' name with a scripture.

In my earlier years, I was Polly's only nephew, before Shane was born, so I was her favourite, notice I say 'was' lol. She saw something in me from a young age and always pushed and helped nurture me. When I was seven years old, three years before I had a dream about God, she buys me a bible for my birthday, a white book. Who does that? What kind of aunty buys their 7-year-old favourite nephew a Bible for their birthday? That's like giving me vegetables instead of birthday cake. But she clearly saw something. I became very acquainted with that bible; it was a simple book for my age range to help understand basic concepts in the Bible and main Bible characters.

So now Polly speaks to me and tells me that if I want siblings, to write it down on the cheque and claim it by faith, this was instrumental to me and my development as a Christian. This helped me to build my faith and trust in God. Two years later my sister was born and eight years later, my brother was born, even when the doctors said that my mom couldn't have any more children.

Life is good now, I'm baptised and filled with God's Spirit, I've just witnessed the power of prayer and seen my aunty Sally come back to church. My mom is now pregnant with my sister 'because of my faith and prayers', my parent's had nothing to do with it lol. Being a Christian is great and life is sweet. At this point, I've never experienced any real struggles or negativity since I was five years old, all this was about to be tested…

Chapter reflections

- *Have you ever had a supernatural encounter, or experienced something that science and logic can't explain? If so, how has this impacted you and your life?*
- *Who are some of the influential people in your life that helped you to succeed and become the person you are today?*

Chapter 4
When Real Life Kicks In

It's still 1997 and now I am in high school, it's a new era and season for me. It's funny, when you're in Junior school, you believe that you will keep the same friends when you get to High School. But those of us who have been to High school, know this to be false in most cases.

In Junior school, as mentioned previously, it was largely made up of white students and very few black students. So when I get to high school, Menzies High school, in West Bromwich, it's refreshing to see a lot more diversity. In large parts, the black kids hanged out with the black kids, the Indians stuck together and the white students stuck together.

I think in every child's life, this stage in high school plays a huge role in a person becoming who they will be for the rest of their life. Not that people don't change from high school, but the experiences we go through will always be in our subconscious and help us make decisions.

Outside of school at the local park by Hill Top, there's a football camp happening every Wednesday. At that time, my grandparents were fostering a young woman, who for the purpose of the story, we'll call Sarah. She was one of the foster kids that I really got on well with, she was like literal family, like an aunty to me, to this day she still keeps in touch with the family.

So, Sarah would take me across the road to this football camp, they had mini matches, penalty shoot outs and different competitions with prizes. I remember one Wednesday my dad came to watch me too, which was rare because of his work away, but something that I liked, every son deep down wants their father to be at events that are important in our own eyes and I was eager to show my dad what I could do. Again, I think every son wants and needs affirmation from their father or a fatherly figure.

> *"... and behold, a voice from heaven [God] said, 'This is my beloved Son [Jesus], with whom I am well pleased.'" Matthew 3:17 (ESV).*

So, we are getting to the end of the schedule for the weekly events, and I get scouted by the son of the manager for a local Sunday league football team, Bustleholme Boys. I'm excited that I was even chosen and so is my dad. In my mind, I thought it was a nice gesture, but I have church on a Sunday at the same time so I can't make it. I decide to try out one match on Sunday after training midweek with the team. Now it's my dad taking me and on this occasion my cousin Charlotte comes.

They decide to play upfront as the main striker in a 4-3-3 formation. It's a great debut! I score the first goal, going one on one with the goalkeeper and sliding it past him. Then I score another goal, I'm outside the box, with my back facing the goal and a defender right behind me. The ball is fed into me bouncing, I chest it to control the ball, then swivel and volley the ball into the back of the net – what a goal! Then to finish it off, I get a penalty for the team, after going round the goalkeeper and been taken down. The captain takes the penalty, scores and we win 3–1. I'm excited, the manager and the players are impressed, my dad is proud, but it's Sunday and I should be at church…

Back in those days, it was almost a capital crime to be somewhere else instead of church, even if you were working a job, let alone playing football. In our church organisation, people weren't even supposed to go to the cinema, it was very strict back then.

I remember walking back to the car, talking to my dad asking him how I am going to tell the team that this was a one off and that I wouldn't be playing again. My dad said we would figure something out. In the end, I tried to do both on a Sunday; go church and play football, after all, there's two services on Sunday, plus a midweek service, two out of three isn't bad – that was my thinking.

On a Sunday morning, I would leave home with my mom and go to church in the morning. With our church in Kelvin Way, West Bromwich, when you walk in the door, you're at the back of the church. Then you have the chairs for the congregation, then the rostrum and the pulpit, where the choir, Ministers and Pastor sat. So I was on the choir, sitting at the top, then in the middle of the service, I would get up where everyone could see me, walk through the entire church, a sort of walk of shame and leave the building and meet my dad, who would be waiting for me in the car park. I hated this, especially when it was a good service where everyone was having a good time, plus, I could just feel people's eyes on me and sense their judgement.

It's funny, because 10 years later, some of the people who were judging me, when their kids are older, they did the same thing and the parents became very defensive when their kids were mentioned in conversation.

"Don't judge someone, especially if you have never experienced the thing that they are going through, because one day, it can happen to you, your children or family."

I've heard so many stories of leaders in church making rules for everyone else, but when it happens to their children or family, all of sudden the rules change… Just saying.

So every Sunday for an entire football season, this was my routine. We get to the end of the season and have an awards ceremony. The main trophies are for 'players player of the season', chosen by all teams mates. Then there was another trophy chosen by the opposition we faced every week for who was the best player on our team, I win both trophies. Each week, our football results and goal scorers are printed in the local newspaper – The Chronicle, Mommy Fletcher would cut out everything with my name and save them.

It had been a great season and I was proud of myself with my results. Sundays were good because it was a bonding experience for me and my dad, especially with him working away all the time. Now the season is over, and I have a decision to make, will I return to Bustleholme and see where football takes me, or do I quit and make this sacrifice and put God first?

After some time, praying and also getting counsel, I decide to make the sacrifice. Even at that age, as much as I loved playing football and believe me, I loved it and had a huge passion for it, I knew I couldn't put anything before my relationship with God.

"I would rather be uncomfortable for a season in God's will, then comfortable with the things I want outside of His will."

My above quote would be a principal that I would learn again later on in life.

I could see that my dad was disappointed with my decision, for a time so was I, but in life, sometimes you just have to make a decision and give your all and this is what I did. I always do think, in a parallel universe, where there's another version of me who carried on playing football; how far would I have gotten? I guess we'll never know, such is life.

When the football season finishes, I am in year 8. At home, my dad is excelling in his career and climbing the ladder and making good money. But now the job requires him to spend time in London and sometimes in other countries away from home, but it seems worth it because of the money. This decision would contribute to the dismantling of my family and would teach me a lesson that I wouldn't have to go through myself.

"Having all the money in the world means nothing if it means losing what's really important."

I believe my dad's intention was to provide a better life for his wife, son and baby on the way, especially having come from humble beginnings. But somewhere down the line, these intentions would morph into something else and produce catastrophic consequences that would remain to this day.

I remember being in year 8, in 1998 and my dad would work away from home Monday to Friday, come back on Friday evening and go back on the Sunday evening. So I never really saw my dad and when he was home, to me, at that age, he was this strict, like a dictator that just created ridiculous rules, even during school holidays – that's how it felt as a 13-year-old boy. So if I wanted to play on the PlayStation in half term or the six weeks holiday, I would have to do an hour of work, to play an hour on the PlayStation. I thought slavery was abolished. This was how my dad was raised and if it was good enough for him, it was good enough for me. If my teachers never gave homework, then my dad was sure to create something for me to do. My grandad Beckford was strict too when raising my dad and aunty Amelia and to be fair, the results don't lie. So now I see why my dad took this approach.

Now that I was no longer playing football, naturally my relationship changed with my dad as we were missing out on that weekly bonding experience – this was something that I loved and missed. Playing well in a football match and knowing that my dad was proud of me was a feeling that I craved, needed and pushed for. Now the only way to make my dad proud was in my school grades.

Although my dad was hardly physically around, he was sure to make up for his absence with money. Looking back, this is definitely my dad's love language in terms of how he shows and gives love. I always had everything I needed in terms of clothes, trainers, games and everything that a teenager wants. As long as I got good grades and performed well in school, I could have anything that I wanted. This shaped my mentality and ultimately contributed to the type of jobs I had and have now – jobs with commission. The harder you work, the more money you earn.

Briefly skipping ahead, my first job was when I was 19, I worked at Showcase cinema in Castlegate Way, Dudley. It was an easy job as you would expect; I had to clean the cinema after each film, then check the quality of all 14 screens by watching a few minutes and making sure the picture and sound was good. The job was cushy and the people were good, but I was highly unmotivated and just didn't care, partly for other reasons that will become evident later on in this journey, but mainly because, from my perspective, there was no incentive. All my life I had been shaped and moulded to understand that the harder you work, the more you get back and rewarded. Now I'm in my first job and I realise that if I turn up late or not, if I'm the hardest worker or not, I will be rewarded and paid the same amount. So what's the point in trying and working hard – that doesn't make any sense. That was my attitude for the four years that I worked there, until I found what I was looking for, a job that matched everything that I had been taught.

Back to me in year 8, 13 years old. At this point in my life, my relationship with my mom was very strong, it always was to be fair. We were Mother and son, but I could talk to my mom as a friend. I felt comfortable talking to my mom about anything and everything, we had and still have a strong bond. This bond only increased at this time, because my mom was now pregnant with my sister Calesha. Finally, my prayer that started a few years is now manifesting, but not before some serious complications.

In the first trimester of the pregnancy, my mom isn't feeling so well and starts bleeding whilst she was at work. She phones the emergency doctor and explains what's happening and the symptoms, after carefully listening to Mom, the doctor responds and tells her that it sounds like she is losing her baby; there's nothing that can be done, go home and make arrangements to get to the hospital for the next steps.

My mom leaves work and sits in the car, tears begin to fall down her face. She doesn't know what to do, then she instinctively calls Mommy Fletcher, the prayer warrior, Mommy Fletcher, the intercessor. She tells Mommy Fletcher what happened on the doctor's call, Mommy Fletcher lets her know that she will start praying.

My mom hangs up the phone and calls my aunty Polly, the faith woman, my aunty Polly who knows that 'the effectual and fervent prayer of a righteous man availeth much'. James 5:16 (KJV). Polly listens to everything that my mom has to say and simply responds, "I'm on it."

"There is something powerful and dangerous about a woman that knows how to pray."

Peace begins to settle in my mom's heart and spirit. All of a sudden, a scripture from the Bible comes into my mom's heart; 'I shall not die, but live and declare the works of the Lord' Psalms 118:17 (KJV). My mom begins to personalise the scripture and declare, "This child shall not die, but live".

My mom starts to stand in the gap and intercedes on behalf of my sister whilst she is in the womb, she speaks these words into the atmosphere for my sister. These words would become my mom's mantra through the pregnancy.

As she sits in the car, with a new perspective and expectation that contradicts everything the doctor has just told her, she puts on her seat belt and begins to make her way to Hill Top. For the entire journey back, my mom is singing 'Great is the Lord and greatly to be praised', with every fibre of her being, expecting God to move mountains, as though my sister is already born.

"... the God who gives life to the dead and calls into being things that were not." Romans 4:17 (NIV)

24 years later (2022) and my sister Calesha, is alive and well, finished university with a 2:1, baptised and filled with God's spirit, a youth leader in the church, leading Bible study on a Sunday morning and on the worship team singing and declaring the works of the Lord – The power of faith and prayer!

In high school, I'm still in year 8, but now I'm beginning to change, now reality and real life is starting to kick in. In year 7, I'll never forget, one of my friends, who I ended up working with 13 years later after the hiring manager asked me what I knew about, for a form of reference; spoke to me and said, "You're different, there's something different about you". I had been in a cocoon for years after being baptised and this relationship with God changed my character and was evident. But during this time, I hadn't really dealt with anything. I guess you could say I was like Adam and Eve in the garden, but before they were tempted and tested.

In high school, no one knew that I was a Christian and I didn't go around shouting about it. Just like when I was in year 1 around mainly white pupils and wanted to fit it, it was the same now, only instead of white pupils, it was pupils that were not baptised, didn't read the Bible and behaved accordingly. Of course as a young person, I wanted to fit in and be like the rest. This really impacted me and my identity – am I a Christian who speaks in tongues or am I just like the other kids. I didn't want to be different. In terms of my identity at the time, I couldn't imagine being a Christian and being different to everyone else, I wasn't brave enough to be different, I couldn't fly in my dreams and as a result, this impacted my reality.

In year 7, the scar on my arm didn't bother me, probably because I was still carrying that child-like mentality from primary school. When we had PE, there were two options, a T-shirt, or a long-sleeved Rugby top. In year 7, I would comfortably wear T-shirts and it was as if I never had a scar on my arm. When I get into year 8, it was like a switch went off in my head and I was very aware now. It was like when Adam and Eve were in the garden naked, but as soon as they disobeyed and ate the fruit, their eyes were opened and they realised they were naked and with that came shame and guilt. I didn't have the guilt, but I had the shame.

I think all teenagers reach that point where they start to become aware of their physical identity, girls start wearing make-up, doing hair and become conscious of their bodies. The boys want regular haircuts, want the latest clothes and want to go to the gym to get muscles. I had reached this point now. From that age, I would only wear T-shirts around people that I felt comfortable with, which was my family as they had always been around me ever since I had the scar. It would just make me feel paranoid that people are staring at my arm, then people would ask questions which made me feel even more uncomfortable. Some people would ask with sensitivity in their voice and there are those who just blurt things out without considering how their words would make me feel.

It just made sense to me to just cover up where possible. There were so many years where I would hate summer, because it would be so hot, that there was no way that I could avoid wearing at least a T-shirt. I learned over time how to walk and where to stand to make sure that my left side wasn't showing or was facing a wall, away from other people's view to this day, this behaviour is just instinctive.

When I got into my twenties and had my first serious relationship, it went on for 18 months and she never knew that I had a scar on my arm and it was never spoken about. This is how much I perfected the art of hiding.

Even recently, during the Covid lockdowns, when we were having BBQs at my house and having family and friends over; on one occasion I had to wear a T-shirt because it was that hot, I would have worn a light shirt if possible. Someone was staring at my scar and I could feel them staring, then they ask what happened to me before blurting out a comment – I got really uncomfortable, my heart starts pounding and I can feel myself starting to get hot, if I was white, I would have turned bright red. This is recently, so imagine how I felt as a young 13-year-old with other identity struggles.

In my high school, it was good because there were more black students, there were about eight black girls in my year and about the same number of black boys. In year 7, I was glad to see this, but as time went on, I began to feel different from the rest of the other black kids – my own people. Firstly, with things like music, they all liked the same things and were a product of their home environments, so music like hip hop, Bashment and jungle music, were conversations I remember hearing. But my environment was gospel music, and no one was talking about that. It was evident that I was the only one who went to church regularly and made a personal commitment. Even with my dad, the type of music that he would listen to was soul and more slow jams and some R&B. But at that age, especially the boys, trying to find their own identity and saying and doing things that look good were into what I called, hardcore hip hop and trying to rap. Meanwhile, I am listening to gospel, getting into the Bible and would preach my first message on a Sunday morning just a few months later when I get into year 9.

I really tried to fit in, I remember one time at lunch time on the playground, I had my Walkman and was playing one of the latest popular hip hop songs. One of the other black boys came up to me and asked what I was listening to, I responded and he gave me a nod and smile of approval – I felt accepted and part of a group, a part of something, so now I have an identity. With my dad not being in church since I was born or can remember, I never had a male role model who was a Christian to look up to. I didn't have anyone to tell me or show me how to be a Christian boy in high school. There were no footprints in the snow for me to walk in, so I had to create my own footprints and I got wet and messed up along the way.

Just as I became aware of my scar now that I am older, the sexual awakening and appetite began to resurface too.

When reality and real-life issues kick in.

Since I was around six years old, the hunger and curiosity had mostly settled down. It wasn't until I was 10 years old that I started to experience puberty, with this came sexual arousal. If I was up late at night, I would see movies or TV shows with sex scenes that caught my attention and left me wanting more, as with most young boys. If you're reading this and you have children and are feeling uncomfortable, then what conversations are you having with your children about sex? Because if you're not talking about this, the school system is, social media is and all the TV soaps and movies on Netflix are definitely doing so.

For me, this is the problem, no one speaks, so every generation starts from scratch, instead of starting from experience and Godly wisdom from the church. I didn't have anyone, especially men in church to teach me about all this...

Although I was baptised at 10 years old, I had no understanding about sex and the Bible, all I knew was that sex before marriage was wrong. In my head, anything except actual penetrative sex was okay. Again, I had no male role models in church to give me a Biblical perspective on sex. So for four years, I watched porn thinking it was okay, because I wasn't actually having sex. Even though I was watching porn, only on TV, this is before internet porn, I lacked understanding. I had no clue what ejaculation was or masturbation, so I would be getting myself all hot and bothered with no output and not knowing that an output existed.

I would watch WWE, at the time it was called WWF wrestling, Monday Night Raw on a Friday evening at 10pm. It was live on Monday in the US but wouldn't air until the Friday. After it finished at midnight, immediately there was 10-minute free view of sex on the same channel, showing naked women, this was something I looked forward to, I was young and curious.

So for four years, from the age of 10 until I was 14 in year 9, this was my life, at church speaking in tongues, but at home watching porn and I thought it was okay, because I wasn't having sex.

"Children raised in Christian homes, should be taught about sex with a Biblical perspective, before they are taught by the school system, their friends, social media or movies."

One day, all the family is at Hill Top after church on Sunday as per usual. Helen makes a comment in jest speaking about something completely different, she says "Well you have thought about it, so you may as well do it, as you have already sinned." I laugh and ask what she means. She explains the Bible verse in Max 5:28 where Jesus explains that if you look at a woman and lust for her in your heart, it's the same as committing the actual act. I couldn't believe what I was hearing, I had to ask her to explain again, maybe I have misheard or misunderstood. She explains again, I am sitting there in utter disbelief. How have I never heard this before? Why was I never taught this bit of crucial information? So watching porn is wrong, even though I'm not doing anything myself?

The year before, when I was 13, all the boys used to talk about was getting a 'shine' from a girl, a shine is another name for oral sex. Again, at this time, in my mind, everything is acceptable except full blown sex. Even with this mentality, I still had no idea about ejaculation, but all I knew is after all this build up from the age of five, all I wanted was a shine. In that year, puberty is still taking place and get my first wet dream and wake up in a mess. My bedroom door was directly opposite my parent's bedroom door and both doors are open, when I roll out of bed, in shock, it's apparent to everyone what happened. I try to rush to the bathroom to clean myself up but Dad sees me, laughs and says, "How was she?" My embarrassment turns to pride, that same smile that my dad would have when I used to play football has reappeared and he seems proud of me, because I'm growing up and experiencing things that young men go through. It was like that nod of approval that I got in the playground from the other black boy who gave me a form of affirmation.

This put me in a weird space as time went on because I wasn't meant to be lusting after women because it's a sin, but I'm a young virile guy, going through puberty having wet dreams. I mean if I'm not horny at this age and attracted to women, wouldn't something be biologically wrong with me? I was confused with who I should be and how I should be feeling.

So I'm 13 years old and want a shine, there's a girl from our school who is promiscuous and well known. She was known for giving shines to a lot of boys. This was a year before I would find out from my gran-aunt Helen that even thinking about a woman is a sin, let alone getting a shine. One day, I'm at Hill Top Park after school, at this stage in my life, this was a normal and regular occurrence, there was a group of other kids, mainly black and Indian from the area that would always meet up at the park to play football or basketball. At the time everyone's age ranged from 12 to about 18.

On this particular day, the girl is there, everyone is playing basketball on the courts. She calls me over, all the guys are smiling and laughing giving nods of approval, just like my dad did when I played football, just like the boy did at school when I was listening to the 'right' music and just like my dad's reaction when I got a wet dream. In this moment, I am really nervous and have no idea what to expect, this something that I've never even seen in porn, I've just heard about it. Because I'm so nervous and practically petrified as I am not ready for this, I'm not even aroused. So why am I doing this? I don't even want this. But it's that need for affirmation I'm craving, it's the identity that I want and think I need to be a 'man' and fit in, just like when I was infant school colouring myself with pink crayons to be like everyone else.

We go behind a bush, at this stage, even though I had a wet dream, I still don't understand what it means to ejaculate. I feel weird, not knowing what to expect and how I should be feeling, totally unaroused without the understanding that the whole purpose is to orgasm. It must have been just a few mins; I just stop as this is going nowhere. We both immerge from the bushes; I get the affirmation and nods of approval that I was looking for. This would be an experience that I wouldn't revisit for some time.

Rumours around school start circulating that I got a shine, it helped 'boost' my reputation and identity. From this age, I had the mentality that I never wanted to be in a relationship with anyone, back then we called it 'checking', so James is checking so and so. I didn't want to give myself to anyone emotionally, this was something that I wanted to save for marriage. This mentality came straight after my first girlfriend in year 8. For the purpose of this exercise, I'll call her Michelle.

I first notice Michelle back in year 7 and was attracted to her for a while. She had Jamaican-Indian hair and wore them in braids. I had never spoken to her, just noticed her. There was a year 7 school disco. I go to the disco and she's there, I'm too nervous to speak to her, what would I even say? I get my friend to ask her out for me, looking back, this was so crazy, we had never spoken but I'm asking her to be my girlfriend – sounds like an arranged marriage. But this was normal back then, I had a girl that I went to Primary school with, come to me earlier in the year and ask me out on behalf of one of her friends.

So my friend proceeds with my request and asks her out. If she would have yes, I don't even know what I would have done, my friend would have had to be the middleman communicator for us. Anyway, I see my friend talking to her whilst the music is playing at the disco. She looks over to me whilst speaking to my friend, now they have stopped talking and now she is walking over to me. This is not part of the plan! What is she thinking? What is she doing? What should I do? I just try to act indifferent as she finally arrives. She says hello and is really polite, the music is pretty loud, so I mostly hear every other word, but I can get the general message. She says she doesn't want to go out with me but wants to be friends, I act cool like I haven't just asked out a girl for the first time in my life and got rejected – this experience would prove useful later on in my life.

A year later, when I'm in year 8, Michelle is back, but now she wants to be my girlfriend, this is great! This is what I wanted in the first place; I knew she couldn't resist me lol. So I now have a girlfriend, the only problem is, we're both shy and don't know how to talk to each other. Back then, people didn't have mobile phones, so you would phone people on their house phone. So I take her number and I remember being in my bedroom at home on the house phone. I call Michelle, say hello, but then I don't have much to say, I've never done this before. This isn't like speaking to my male friends, this is my girlfriend, so surely our conversations should be different… right? The call goes terrible. Back at school, we hardly speak to one another because we are both so shy. The next time I called her, I would try to be as prepared as possible, I write a list of conversation starters, to ensure there's no awkward silences. The conversation goes great, we both feel more relaxed and the conversation is flowing nicely – now we're cooking!

Weeks go by, but we still haven't had our first kiss. Earlier that same year, there was another school disco. By this time, I had started to make forms of relationships with the "black girls" in my year, this is what they were referred as. At the disco, they were playing 'Truth or Dare', I was dared to kiss one of the black girls, one of Michelle's friends, this would be before Michelle and I started 'checking'. I had no experience in kissing, I didn't know any techniques or anything. So Michelle's friend comes up to me for the dare, we both just stand there for a few moments, waiting for the other person to start, then she just starts, she's not just kissing, she's French kissing, I just freeze like a deer in the headlights. Most people close their eyes when they kiss, my eyes were wide open and it's like I'm having an out of body experience. "So this is kissing? What do I do with my tongue? I'll just try writing the alphabet or something with my tongue." It seemed like a long kiss, over a minute, I want to say that 'we' stopped, but I was literally a passenger in this situation.

Sometime later, following this year 8 school dance, Michelle's friend would tell her friends that I didn't know how to kiss – she wasn't lying. So now, we're back in the present and I'm dating Michelle but not had our first kiss. There's a dance happening in West Bromwich, by the old swimming baths called 'The Lick', it was really a 'Black' event. At this event, Michelle and I are relatively good in our relationship, the only thing missing is the first kiss and now she's going on holiday soon and wants a kiss before then.

I'm at the party with some friends from school, some of the other black boys. Michelle comes over to me whilst I'm talking to my friend. She asks if we can go outside to talk, all three of us knew that was code for "it's time". I felt a bit nervous, as I didn't want to disappoint her like I did with her friend. But at the same time, I'm feeling fairly confident now. You see, earlier that week or month, I had a dream where we kissed, the dream was almost like a training room where I practised my technique. So now, all I have to do is replicate what I did in my dream – copy and paste.

We go outside and walk around the corner, there's small talk, "tonight's been good, the music was on point" etc… More small talk continues, whilst our eyes are having their own conversation. As Chris Rock famously once said in one of his comedy routines, "A lot of first kisses come in the middle of a conversation… it's like double Dutch (skipping ropes), you're just waiting to jump in." Just like Chris Rock said, we were in the middle of the conversation, unlike at the school dance with her friend, this time, I wouldn't wait, now I got confidence because I learned to fly (kiss) in my dreams, so now I believed I could do the same in reality. We kiss and it's great, just as I had practised in my dreams.

Sometime later, we would break up before I went into year 9 and turned 14. I believe there was a disagreement, and we went our separate ways. It was at this point that I decided not to get into any more relationships. I didn't see the point in investing my time, emotions and energy into something that wouldn't result in marriage. In my mind, one day, because we know this isn't forever, a relationship would just stop and breakdown, so what's the point?

At that age, I didn't know what the rules were in church about having boyfriends and girlfriends. It certainly wasn't mentioned or discussed at my church, and it wasn't really spoken about in my church's organisation, not that I had ever heard. So this added to my confusion about my identity and what I can and can't do.

> *"I really wished back then that I had a male role Christian model to help me navigate through my life."*

Chapter Reflections

- *What sacrifices have you had to make in life and how do you feel about your decision(s)?*
- *What was your relationship like with your parents growing up and what would you change if you could?*
- *How old were you when 'real life kicked in'? What was the situation and how did it impact you?*

Chapter 5
Purpose – Revealed, Received, But Not Registered

I'm now in year 9 and 14 years old and we are entering into a new millennium. Everything at school is going fine, I'm still in all the tops sets for my subjects, my dad is still strict as ever. Normally, teachers put pupils on report for bad behaviour or other negative reasons, but it's my dad who requested for me to be on report so that I'm closely monitored for my work and behaviour. Back then, I didn't understand why my dad was like this, but as I got older it became clearer to me. He wanted to make sure I was getting the most out of school and also to make sure that he was getting the most out of my teachers.

One time, in my biology class, as part of punishment for my behaviour, my teacher gave me lines to do. Lines is where you write something like, "I will not misbehave in class again," but you would write it like a hundred times. My dad was not happy with this, so one of the weeks when he was in the Midlands, he came to my school and had a meeting with my teacher and I. He told him he didn't want me writing lines as a punishment, he would much rather have me doing some kind of report or project where I can learn something. This parenting style is something that he got from my grandad Beckford and was a huge factor in his own career.

All my friends would ask why my dad came and was so strict. I remember back when I was in Year 8, I had parents evening, I had booked appointments with all my teachers. It was a pretty decent evening overall. I remember my dad saying to me, "Did you see all the other parents, how they were dressed and the cars they drove?" He wasn't being materialistic; he was drawing a comparison with the other parents and he and my mom. He was explaining that the decisions that all the parents made back in high school contributed to who they became.

Without saying it, he was saying, "Who do you want to be in 20 years and what type of lifestyle do you want?"

"The decisions we make now contribute to what our life will be tomorrow – decide wisely!"

This helped, as it made me see the big picture and also have ambition. A lot of the pupils in my school didn't have a successful role model in terms of a job and career. I'm grateful that I had this.

In church, I would become part of the Youth Department as the Vice President and my aunty Sally was President. There were three departments in our church and every other church in the organisation, Bethel, founded by Bishop Sydney Alexander Dunn, the presiding Bishop at the time. There was the Youth, Men's and Women's department. Each department had their own Sunday in a month, where they would lead service and provide the preaching. Second Sunday of the month was Women's Sunday and people wore white, third Sunday was Men's or Brotherhood Sunday, people would wear shades of blue. Lastly, fourth Sunday was Youth Day and people would wear red and black, other Sundays were a generic day where anyone could lead the services.

It was during this year that I would preach my first message on a Sunday morning, it was taken from 1 Samuel chapter one. I don't recall the title, but the theme was to do with sacrifice and being willing to give up the things you love most for God, just like I had done the year before with my football career, if I can even call it that.

It was around this time that I had another LCI. I don't know what caused it, why it started or exactly when, but every time that I had to do anything at church, I would get extremely nervous to the point where I would literally vomit. But it wasn't just at church, the family's Monday night prayer meeting was still going strong, following its conception four years earlier. Even when I was just around my family, if they asked me to read, pray or speak, I would run to the downstairs bathroom and vomit. Anything remotely to do with church or God, I would become paralysed with fear. So of course, I dreaded going to church and prayer meetings. In my church at that time, as was the case in most of the branches, you could walk into church and then be told you are the service leader, preacher or called to pray in front of the whole church with no notice. Every Saturday night, I would have butterflies and fear would start to build.

There were a few times in church, where I would get nervous and run out of church to the toilet to vomit, but there were sometimes that I just never made it to the toilet in time. Other people would clean up my vomit, I would feel so embarrassed and ashamed. Maybe it's best if no one calls me, maybe it's best that I never speak again. In fact, I don't want to speak again, this is too much and I don't want this.

"Often times, the area of your pain, is the area of your power and calling."

Despite everyone knowing that I had this issue, it didn't stop people at church calling me to do things. They saw a gift in me and the church would help me develop this whether I liked it or not, today I can say that I'm grateful for this.

At this time, no one would push me more than my aunty Sally, it's like the women in my family were carrying a baton, this baton represented pushing me, encouraging me and making me the best version of myself; this baton was now with Sally.

Sally, like Polly and Mommy Fletcher was like a second mother. If I spoke to my mother, I could safely assume that Sally knew. Because Sally was the younger sister to my mom she was like a cool aunty and older sister all in one. I would talk to Sally like I would speak to my mom and she was absolutely hilarious, she could literally be a comedian.

We worked together on the youth team and set up separate meetings for the youth, where we would have pizza nights and watch captivating Gospel videos, at the time it was a series called 'The Truth Behind Hip Hop' by G. Carter Lewis.

She would practically force me to preach either on a Sunday morning or Sunday Night and I would literally beg her to leave me alone, but she would tell me that I have a gift to speak, and the gift wasn't for me to sit on, but to help others. Sometimes tough love is needed, and you need to be seemingly cruel to be kind.

So I was stuck, I was apparently gifted and called to preach, but every time I was called to preach, I would vomit. It was in this season that I had to adapt my approach to church. Before I would wake up and come to church with a casual mindset, so when fear came on me, I would vomit. Now, I would fast on a Sunday and another day in the week. On Sunday morning, I would start praising and worshipping as soon as I got up. I would now learn to worship at home. Just like when I was 10 years old at the altar on the Sunday morning of my baptism – I would give everything, no complacency. I found that when I worshipped, there was an atmosphere of God's presence and the Bibles says:

> *"... and where the Spirit of the Lord is, there is freedom."*
> *2 Corinthians 3:17 (ESV)*

When I was in worship, I was free from fear because I was full of God. Just like a car occupying a car space and there's no space for another car – this was me. This was my protection, my shield, my comfort, my hiding place and the place that I ran to in my times of need. As a by-product of me always being in this state, the anointing, God's power would flow through me so that whatever I was doing came with power and authority, where others see something in me.

> *"I thought I needed God to help me get through this trial, but God was using this trial to bring me to the point where he wanted me to be."*

I've heard people say you should only thank God in the trial but not for the trial, but I can genuinely say, I'm grateful for this particular trial. It changed the trajectory of my spiritual life and is the reason why I am who I am. Everything for a reason!

When I was 14, some of the family would go to Canada to visit Mommy Fletcher's sister and family, auntie Sonia. Her son was getting married, and we were invited. It was me, my parents and Calesha, who was around 1 year old, Sally and her two girls, Rachel and Shabeena, who we call Shabz; Helen, her granddaughter Josephine and her foster son Gary and Mommy and Daddy Fletcher. This would start of the series of family holidays that would take place annually, which would gradually grow to 22 people.

Although this was meant to be holiday and a wedding occasion, it certainly didn't feel that way. Auntie Sonia and Uncle Lloyd pastored a church, which meant that we were always at church most days. The day we landed, although we had jet lag, we had to go to church, although I was a Christian, I wasn't happy with this, even in the garden of Eden, Adam had time to chill before God came down in the cool of the day. There was one occasion where we went on a day trip which incorporated several hours of driving, in two cars where we were all packed in like sardines in a tin. We get to our destination for this day trip, then auntie Sonia announces we are going to church, we were all shocked. In the churches that we all went to, women had to wear a hat and cover their heads. This was immediately fired back to auntie Sonia after she announced that we were going to church. One of the women said, "But we don't have any hats to wear, so how can we go?" Auntie Sonia calmly walked to the boot of her car, popped it open to show an array of hats, with this, all excuses were taken away, so we go church.

At this stage of my life, my mindset would fluctuate very easily from a dedicated Christian who loves to fast and pray to a mindset where I just want to be a regular teenager and 'enjoy life'. In Canada, it was the later mindset that was currently prevailing.

On another day, we go out again, then get told that we are going to church again, my dad who's not in church is angry as he feels he's been set up – join the club. We go to this church and there's a man from USA there teaching, his name is Dr Jefferson. But this guy is no ordinary preacher, I've never heard the Bible preached and taught in this way. He's able to bring things to life in the simplest way and makes your spirit hungry for God. It wouldn't be long until his reputation reaches the UK, and he becomes a regular preacher in all Bethel churches as well as the main speakers at Bethel's annual convention where all Bethel churches from around the world meet up. His preaching helped me so much from that point up until I was 19, to this day I still remember his messages; 'Dreamer vs Dream maker', 'Delayed but not denied', 'Anointed to die', just to name a few. This was one the first time that I was happy to be at church whilst I was on holiday.

One of the evenings, we all got to aunties Sonia's church, everyone gives strict instructions not to call them to do anything as we all just want to relax. The service goes on, against everyone's wish, auntie Sonia call Helen and Mommy Fletcher to give a short exhortation, neither of the two are prepared or impressed. They go up to speak, my mom and Sally are sitting in their seats looking and feeling smug. Auntie Sonia goes back into the pulpit; she requests a short rendition of a song before announcing that the next voice you will hear will be the main speaker of the night… Audrey Beckford. I was shocked and nervous for my mom, so I can only imagine how she feels. She goes up and preaches and does really well but isn't happy.

Whilst I was there, because I was only 14, I was pretty much ignored by the church members as their attention went to the 'adults'. Then one night, this would all change, this would be the night where my purpose would be revealed and received.

"Revealed, received, but not registered."

On a night that we went back to auntie Sonia's church, they had a guest speaker that had been there before, he was just 18 years old, his name was Kevin Smith. To this day, after 25 years plus in church, I have never heard a more anointed preacher than him. He was heavily, heavily gifted.

Uncle Lloyd gets into the pulpit to introduce him before he preaches and talks about his bio and credentials, I remember specifically that Uncle Lloyd said that Kevin had prophesied many times and everything that he had said always came to pass.

Kevin preaches like only he can preach; he starts doing an altar call for anyone who wants prayer. He looks in my direction and says, "You, come here." Surely, he can't be speaking to me, I'm nobody, just some 14-year-old boy, I'm the guy that everyone has been ignoring. He indicates that it's me that he is speaking to. I walk down to the altar. I stand before him as he looks down from the altar and begins to speak before he prophesies over my life. He says that he can see an angel watching over me, indicating that I have favour with God. Then he begins to prophesy in front of everyone, I don't remember it all, neither do my family, I don't know why I nor anyone wrote it down, but what we all remember is:

"You're going to do things and say things that are on another level. People will marvel. You're going to do things that people don't understand and you will excel and overtake and people are going to wonder how you did it."

He then begins to pray for me as tears run down my face and my mindset shifts back to dedicated Christian. Purpose has now been revealed in this prophecy, it's received but it's not registering in terms of understanding of the things that I will do that no one understands. In what way will I excel and overtake? It's not registering. I wouldn't hear anything or observe any sign of this prophecy until another ten years later.

That same night, Kevin prophesies over my auntie Sally too. At the end of the service, previously no one spoke to me or even acknowledged me, now I was the best thing since sliced bread and everyone was speaking to me. It became a joke the family would recall and say every time we spoke about Canada.

Because of this prophecy, mixed with the fact that my family told auntie Sonia that I could preach, they were trying to get me to speak at one of the services. The night Kevin prophesied over me would be the last time I went to church on the holiday, I would make myself unavailable.

Going to Canada helped me to refocus on church and in turn life as a whole, I felt like there was something for me to do and achieve in life now, I just didn't know what it was yet. This would be the start of me constantly looking for this prophesy to be fulfilled. Whenever an opportunity came about in my life, I would quietly question and pray, wanting to know if this what Kevin was speaking about. I would take this quest back to the UK and pursue it.

Chapter Reflections

- *Do you have things in your life that you know you were born to do and complete, but you face huge obstacles? If so, what are you doing about it?*
- *Do you have people in your circle that push you in life to get the best out of you? If so, how are you responding when they push you?*
- *Have you evert received insight into who you are meant to be and the purpose for your life? If so, what have you done since receiving this?*

Chapter 6
Show Me Your Friends and I'll tell You Who You Are

My mom would always repeat this quote (chapter title), it's something that my great grandmother, Mama would always say.

> "... But there is a friend who sticks closer than a brother." Proverbs 18:24 (NKJV)

Between the ages of 14 and 16, I would create some of my strongest friendships, a lot of these friends I consider to be my brothers, some still continue up until now, for the purpose of this exercise, other names will be used. At 14, where we are now in the timeline, my main friend was my future cousin Noah. He joined my Primary school in year 5, as he along with his mother and sister moved into a house literally across the street from the school. It was nice to have another black boy in my year at the time. We became instant friends.

One day, I was at my aunty Amelia's house, my dad's sister. I was there for the day to hang out with my cousin Charlotte. Because Charlotte was mainly around Max and I, more so Max at this point; all the things that we liked, Charlotte was into, even things like football.

As I sit down watching TV, the doorbell goes and I'm asked if I can open the door. I begin to open the door, as it gets halfway open, I instantly recognise that it's Noah from school. We both look at each other shocked, both thinking then verbally asking, "What are you doing here?" I explain that it's my auntie's house and that I'm here often and always have been. I ask him why here is there, he states that he has come to see his dad. At the time, Amelia was dating Geoff, who she would go on to get married around 10 years later. Noah and I couldn't believe it, we're not just friends, we're practically family. This was a friendship that would continue into our twenties, but as is the case in life, we would drift apart, mainly due to my second job that I took on when I was 24 which pretty much alienated me from everyone, including family.

Another key friendship that I would have was with Liam, he started school with me in year 10 when I was 15 years old after moving from Trinidad with some of his family. He stayed with his cousins Dean and Dale; they were all like brothers.

Liam was quiet but highly respected by everyone, even at that young age. There was something different about him. I would find out that he was also a Christian, with a very similar background to me in terms of passion for and knowledge of the Bible. You would think that having Liam there would have made my life easier, but by that time I was back to having a fluctuating mindset again where one day I was a committed Christian and another day I was a regular 15-year-old with only thing on my mind. Looking back, Liam must have thought the English Christians are so much different than Trinidadian Christians. This was a friendship that would grow and remains to this day. We both stayed at Menzies and went to 6th Form, after that we went our separate ways academically.

Three years later, Liam would get married, I was shocked and honoured when he reached out to me and invited me. I just thought that because we hadn't seen each other in a while, that we would just drift apart. Liam would play two pivotal roles in my life by inviting me to two events that would contribute to my life decisions and the aftereffects. If you have a friend like Liam in your life, consider yourself blessed; I have a lot of time, love and respect for Liam, the man from Trinidad.

Amo was a friend that I made at Menzies High School back in year 8. This too is a friendship that has gone the distance and lasted up until now. Our friendship really grew to the point where we went to the same 6th form and then the same university taking all the same classes, at university, Amo was the only person I knew. Normally when people go to university, it's all about new experiences and meeting new people, I was fortunate not to have to go through this alone, as I had Amo and my cousin Ashton. Ashton wasn't in any of our classes as he studied something completely different, but we would frequently meet up at university and I would be the driver that took Amo and Ashton to university with me. They lived five minutes apart and went to primary school together, so already knew each other from then and again in 6th form, when Ashton moved there.

My friendship with Amo was unique as a lot of friendships are based on similarities, particularly when it comes from ethnic and cultural backgrounds, but this was a friendship that would transcend all of this. Amo would invite me to his house, but not other black boys, I would meet and speak to his parents and even greet his grandmother; she didn't speak much English, so we would wave and smile at each other. She would speak Punjabi and Amo would translate. She was keen to make sure that Amo was taking care of me and offered me a drink and food whenever I was there. I really loved that about his grandmother because she was coming from a time where racism would have been high and the perception and opinion of black people would have been low, but she treated me well and I never overlooked that.

Amo's parents were glad that we were friends and for my 'influence' on their son academically. All the strictness that I had received from my dad, was now coming in handy. Later in life, just like Liam, Amo would get married in his early twenties. He invited me and most of our friends from high school. It was my first Indian wedding, the drinks never stopped coming, I was around 24 at this time. Now Amo and I probably speak twice a year, but whenever we have met up, it's like we have always been talking. He was and is a good friend to me and big part of my life growing up.

Whilst at university, Amo and I were in our first Economics lesson, we both chose the same subjects that we took at 6th form – Economics and Business Studies. As we get into groups, we meet Ricky, he's from London and is living in Birmingham in university dorms whilst studying. We all instantly hit off and become inseparable for the next three years at university.

Ricky is the best of both worlds, he is street, with street smarts but also an academic genius. Even the way he spoke and formed arguments over things like football. This became ever evident in his grades, whilst Amo and I got mediocre results, Ricky just excelled. We would ditch class many times to go back to Ricky's dorm or my house to play Pro Evolution Soccer 5 on the PlayStation. We had our own score sheet to keep record of how many matches each person won. I would be behind and ridiculed for three years straight before on the last day of university where we would all go our sperate ways, I would finally turn it all around and become the overall winner, a story that we still talk about whenever we would meet up.

After university, we would only see each other on social media, which wasn't that often, but we would reconnect properly some 10 years later at my stag do.

Ashton, like Noah is a cousin and friend, second cousin to be exact, but who's counting. My dad and his dad are cousins and our mothers are very close too. One of my first memories of Ashton was when I was around six years old, all six of us went to Florida, it was Ashton's parent's honeymoon, I vaguely remember the wedding day. Around this age, we would spend a lot of time at their flat in West Bromwich, which was located near Lodge Road; before they would move into their house on Hope Street, just off Beeches Road. I enjoyed going round there, I would play with Ashton, his sister and their many, many cousins.

After junior school, I would lose touch with Ashton, whilst our parents maintained their relationship. It wasn't until Ashton moved to Menzies 6th form that our friendship properly started. At this time, we were different people that we both previously knew of each, we were older, I wouldn't say mature lol.

As previously mentioned, Ashton would join Amo and I at University and carpool with us. He too became friends with Ricky and the four of us would often hang out. Ashton wasn't into football and playing Pro Evolution Soccer, but there to socialise. After University, Ashton would join me at my second job which was an adventure in and of itself; here our friendship would really grow. Ashton is one of the loyalist people that I know with a huge heart, everyone loves Ashton! You can't not like him. He's that friendly guy who's always smiling. He has remained in my life on a consistent basis to this day. If I needed help or support, he would be one of the people that I would call.

I grew up with my cousin Max in my earlier years, again, he just 11 days older than me. Because of how our birthdays fall, he being born on the 23rd August and me on the 3rd September, we were in different years at school, he was one of the youngest in his year, whereas I was one of the oldest in my year.

Up until the age of around seven years old, I spent a lot of time with Max and my cousin Charlotte. Similar to my relationship with Ashton, there was a gap where the relationship became almost dormant. It wasn't until high school that we reconnected, and our relationship started up again.

In high school, it would be Noah, Max, Charlotte and I that would have what we called FIFA Fridays, where we would all meet at Charlotte's house and play tournaments. Although we went to the same school, we didn't really spend time together as we both had our own friends, this was same with Charlotte and I after she moved to Menzies part way through the high school years.

After college, Max would do a lot of travelling to various African countries for weeks or months at a time, so of course no one saw him in these periods. After my younger years, Max and Charlotte were more like brother and sister and were certainly closer to each other than me; I guess because I spent all my time at Hill Top, my relationship grew with this side of my family significantly more than the other. This would largely remain the case until 2020 when tragedy would bring my sister and I closer to the Beckford side of the family.

In high school, Max's closest friend was a guy called Aiden. I knew of Aiden previously as we went to the same primary school together along with the Rooneys, they were a black family who lived round the corner from Mommy and Daddy Fletcher's house. All the black parents and grandparents in that area of Hill Top knew each other and some had good relationships. There were times where my grandparents were working, so after school, Abigail and I would go round the corner to Mr and Mrs Black' house. They looked after their grandchildren Stacey and Jermaine. Stacey was in my year and we were in the same class at Primary school when I was in year 6.

My grandparents also got on with the Rooneys too. When I was infant school, my nan would pick me up from school, on many occasions, she would also pick up the Rooney's youngest son Mark and his friend Aiden – this is the same Aiden that Max was close friends within High School. So again, I had known of Aiden but never really spoken to him.

One day at school, I believe I was in year 8, it's non-uniform day and school has now finished. Aiden had come to school wearing a T-shirt but no coat. I don't remember what I was wearing, but it was warm enough to not have my coat on and still be fine. The weather begins to change and gets colder. It must have been a dinner time on the courts, this is where people went to play football or basketball. Aiden complains that he's cold, so I offer him my coat as a gesture to help. He accepts and takes this a huge sign of respect and his opinion of me changes, not that I knew he already had one. I started spending more time with Max and Aiden, along with Noah. As time goes by, we see that we have a lot in common and get on well, but at this stage, this is Max's friend.

A couple of years go by, I am in the zone when it comes to church, Max is also fully committed and now Aiden is also, after getting baptised in our organisation around 16 years old. His father was a Pastor of a church from a different denomination and had different beliefs to Bethel, the organisation that Max and I belonged to. The three of us were inseparable between the time when I was 16 years old up until I was 19 years old, especially when it came to church.

As the rest of my story will show, Aiden not only became my best friend, but was a huge part of my life for large portions. He was like a literal brother, even addressing my mom as 'Mom'. The thing that I loved about Aiden was that he was just real, no filter. He made you feel comfortable to just be yourself without fear of judgement. In fact, in my life, he would constantly tell me to stop caring what other people think and just live my life. Over the next 15 years plus, we would spend a lot of time at each other's house, where the other person was treated liked they lived there by other family members. At this stage in my life, I was quite naïve, whereas Aiden had streets sense – he would often say that I was the smartest person with no common sense that he knew. He would become like an older brother to me. He himself had an older brother, so everything that he learned, he would teach me. Finally, I had a male role model, who had a church background and a worldly background, who would contribute to my identity at the time.

Like all my other friends, we too had relatively dormant patch, when I started my second job, but as previously stated, this applied to everyone in my life. But we would reconnect again after that period.

These were the main friends that I had at this time in my life in high school leading up to university. I'm grateful for each and every one of them, good friends are hard to come by.

Chapter Reflections

- Who were some of the best friends that you ever had? Are you still in touch, if not, why not?
- Do you make an effort to reach out to people that you used to be close to? If not, why not?
- What characteristics about your friends do you like?

Chapter 7
Transitions

When I get back from Canada, I'm really focused because of the prophecy in my life. When I go back to school, I start year 10 and I'm now 15 years old. The year was 2001, only a few days into the school year and 9/11 would take place in USA where Osama Bin Laden would take credit for the hijacked planes that crashed into the twin towers. I remember being in an English lesson the day after and my teacher explaining the magnitude of what had just taken place. Because it was in another country and I only saw what happened on TV, it didn't feel real. At this age, I guess you could say that I lived a very sheltered life and never dealt with tragedy, I hadn't even experienced a death in my family on either side. My life was like a Disney film where everything was perfect and bad things didn't happen, in this context and stage of my life. This mentality would both blind and protect me from truth that was in front of me, but the blindness wouldn't stop for another four years.

Elsewhere in the world, the world was introduced to Shrek and donkey for the first time, P Diddy and J Lo had broken up after three years and Aaliyah, the R&B singer tragically died in a plane crash and Apple introduced their first iPod.

The year before at school, we had to choose the subjects that we wanted to study in preparation for our upcoming GCSEs exams we would take in year 11 before we left school. I chose Business Studies, separate sciences, Geography, German, as well as the other mandatory subjects. At this stage, I didn't have a clue what I wanted to be when I would be older, all I knew was that it would be something to do with Business, this was because it was the same field that my dad's work fell into. Career wise, I wanted to be like my dad, high paying job, company car and the big bucks.

In school, I was always in the top sets for each subject; except for subjects like PE or DT which weren't based on academic capability. Set 1 was the top set for the most intelligent pupils. My lowest set was Set 2. Although my dad was strict and tried to monitor my work and behaviour, I still found ways to 'do my own thing', where I wouldn't work at all, or just gave my teachers attitude. I was intelligent with a smart mouth, ready to have a battle of wits with both other pupils, but especially teachers. This meant that in certain subjects like RE and German, my teachers thought that I would amount to nothing academically and fail my GCSEs.

With German GCSEs, it was made up of a listening exam, where they would play a tape of someone speaking German and we had to interpret; but also was comprised of coursework. That year I handed in my German coursework for my GSCEs and got an 'A' grade. My teacher was quick to accuse me of cheating when she handed me my coursework back. I thought she was joking at first, but she confirmed that she was deadly serious. Looking back, I can see how she came to that conclusion, as it appeared that I didn't pay attention in class or show any signs of intelligence. It just so happened that when I was writing up my coursework, that I was in the mood and my creative juices were flowing. Add to that, the conversation my parents had with me following my year 8 parents evening, where I was asked the question, "What type of lifestyle do you want when you're older." Incorporate that with Daddy Fletcher's success culture and mantra of 'You're a Fletcher', I could only succeed. Plus, an incentive was put in place in year 10, ahead of my GCSES results that I would get the following year. For every 'A' grade, I would get £X, and for every 'B' grade I would get £X. There's that "the harder you work, the more you get back" mentality been poured into me and shaping me to help make future life decisions.

In church, things are still going well, I am speaking regularly and working on my gifting in terms of speaking. I'm maturing and going from speaking like a boy, to speaking like a man. At church, we were previously at Kelvin Way, West Bromwich. Now Bethel, after saving for a period have enough money to move ahead with their goal of building a better convention centre.

I remember years prior, Bishop Dunn and his team talking about this goal and sharing the vision, now we're at a place where we're ready to execute. The only problem is, our church called the West Bromwich branch, were having church in the same building. This meant we would have to leave and find someone else to have church.

When the plans for the new building started, our pastor and leaders were on the lookout for another church. Eventually, we found a church on the border of

West Bromwich and Great Bridge. The church had a very old style to it with wood making up most of the interior, including the seats which were very hard and uncomfortable. As we only rented the church, it meant there were restrictions; towards the end of our services, the 'caretaker' would turn up at the back of the church jingling his keys to indicate to us to wind down and finish. He couldn't lock up and go until we all left. In a church with a Jamaican culture, this was hard to adapt to, as there were times when worship was taking place and people needed this atmosphere and additional prayer for whatever their situation was, but this was no longer possible.

That same year, Kevin, the preacher who had prophesied over me, came to England and to our church to preach. At that time, there was a man called Dr Cawley who was from Canada. He was the one that preached when my auntie Sally came back to church. Every year, he would come to the UK, for his annual revival meeting in All Saints, Wolverhampton church. Most years, he would bring other young and upcoming preachers and send the out to different churches in the Bethel organisation to preach the word and I imagine for experience.

This year, Kevin was sent to our church, he would have been 18 or 19 years old, but had the anointing and power of a seasoned 50-year-old experienced preacher. Every time he preached, the atmosphere changed, and people were impacted. In the 25 years plus, since I was baptised at 10 years old, I have never ever heard anyone preach and demonstrate so much anointing and power, that's people I have seen in person and tele-evangelists. I remember one of Dr Cawley's other protégés saying, "Kevin has more anointing in the tip of his little finger, than I have in my whole body," and this was coming from another great preacher.

Kevin being around at that stage in my life helped me focus, but at the same brought on more temptation for me as a young guy. The closer I got to God, the more temptation would come. It would be the same process over and over again, struggle with lust and porn during the week, or at least up to Friday; I had this mentality that I couldn't sin on the Saturday as it was the day before Sunday and the 'smell' of sin and it's affects might become apparent to everyone. Then come to church on Sunday, hear a word, get convicted in my heart and promise never to do it again.

"... For I have the desire to do what is good, but I cannot carry it out. For I do not do the good (that) I want to do, but (the) evil I do not want to do – this I keep on doing." Romans 7:18–19 (NIV)

At this stage in the world, society was at a place where everybody would own their own mobile phone, before this year, it was largely people using their house phones. The phone that had just come out the year before was the Nokia 3310, this would be my first phone. No internet, no camera, no touch screen, no social media platforms, just a brick of a phone, with polyphonic ring tones and the famous game – Snakes. I say all this, because if I had all the things that we have available today in terms of access to anything and everything that you want at a touch of a button, I would have fed my lust from temptations with these things. But living at that time, it would have to be the real thing.

Later in the school year, I would begin to 'See' a girl from the year below, because remember, I don't do relationships anymore. At this stage of my life, I was just a horny teenager who watched porn but never 'released' – this is a lot of build-up. I remember being in a Business Studies class and two of the boys were talking about masturbation and asked me if I do it. In my head, I didn't have a clue what they were talking about and definitely not how to do it. But I just responded and said, "Nah, I don't." They looked at me like I was mad and with a look of disbelief. They thought I was lying and couldn't believe that a teenager our age has never tried or not addicted to it. But again, I had no understanding of how all this worked, all I knew was that I was crazy horny and very curious.

With the girl I was seeing, the sole purpose of us seeing each other was because she was a girl who gave 'shines'. Despite learning two years prior that it's wrong to even look at a woman and lust after her in your heart, I had cognitive dissonance and convinced myself that anything and everything up to penetrate sex was okay. Besides, it wasn't my fault that I was abused, and my sexual appetite and curiosity was opened 10 years ago at just five years old. How does anyone expect me to be horny for all this time with no release and expect me not to do anything. Plus, I had no mentors or anyone to guide me, so my word was the ruling authority.

As I was seeing this girl, unlike my first experience when I was in year 8, I felt more confident and definitely hornier to get a shine, only thing was, I still lacked understanding about how things worked like ejaculation. Back then, porn came in the form of magazines on the shop self, the porn on TV didn't show everything, like it would a few years later on the internet. So I had no reference or a clue about a complete sexual experience and most people around me were virgins.

Rumours began circulating about me seeing this girl for one reason, there more rumours that she had already given me what I wanted – which was false. The rumours gave me a reputation that I liked and gave me respect among my peers. It gave me identity – I was the man…

That year, we had a school talent show and me and the girl that I was seeing agreed to meet up before the show to do the deed, but she never showed up. We speak the next day, and she gives me some excuse as to why she was late and never made. Out of frustration, I end what we had and develop a mentality that I would use over the next 15 plus years, where if a girl was annoying me, I would just let her go as I'm not meant to be sinning in the first place.

In that same year, one of the boys in my year Michael, has moved house and is now living in Hill Top, so after school, he joins Noah and I as we walk home from school. One day, he mentions that he has a 'flex', a flex is a link or girl that you would go and see, because that's what 'real men' did at that age. You were judged by how many girl's numbers you had and how many flexes that you could call on. This flex is in Russell Hall, Dudley and would require three buses and around an hour and a half to get to, depending on how soon the bus came.

There were a group of girls that lived there, and Noah and I would be introduced, we hung out in the park and this massive open field. At that age, that was our first flex, it was exciting and something new. We all got on really well with everyone, there were some girls that liked Noah and some girls that liked me. They were the same age as us or the year below, they would drink alcohol and smoke weed and cigarettes, this was something that Noah and I weren't into, we were there for the girls only.

The friendships with the Russell Hall girls was a friendship that would last for a few years, go dormant and then start back up again when I would get my first job when I was 19/20 years old. When I was 15 years old, going to Russell Hall, although I personally didn't engage form of any sexual activity, the environment and relationships were still something that satisfied my appetite and curiosity.

As I turn 16 years old and enter into year 11 ready for GCSES and then to leave High school, most people will go on to college where you have more freedom and less accountability from teachers and lecturers, but I already know that I will stay at Menzies and got to their 6th form higher education – I was very serious about my future.

In this year, just like every other year, my mentality would continue to fluctuate between committed Christian and regular horny teenager. My friendship with Aiden had got stronger, at this time Noah, Max, Aiden and I were all close. Aiden would become interested in getting baptised which would materialise the next year. Max and I were committed Christians at the time and Noah would go on to be interested but not commit. I don't think my fluctuating lifestyle helped him in his decision making.

During this time period, when I was fluctuating and now with a committed Christian mentality, I wanted to exercise my faith. I was at Hill Top, I had recently opened a bank account as I had turned 16 years old. There was no money in my bank, but I wanted to test my faith. History had shown me the power of faith, coupled with prayer and fasting, but I didn't want to live on the glory of yesteryears. I prayed to God and asked for £10, I thought I would start small, to be in the account. I leave the house and walk to the local shop which has a cash machine in there. It's about a 10-minute walk, this gives me the opportunity to pray more, move by faith and speak things into existence.

"The tongue has the power of life and death…" Proverbs 18:21

So I'm walking to the shop and I'm believing God and thanking God for this money. In my mind, I am convinced that there £10 in my account now and no one can tell me any different. I arrive at the shop; I take my bank card out of my tattered Adidas wallet. I insert the card into the cash machine, whispering words of faith and praise under my breath. As I put the pin in, I turn my eyes away from the screen whilst the machines load up my balance… I slowly turn my head and eyes to the direction of the screen with expectation… and… the balance says… £0.00. I'm fuming and confused, why hadn't this worked? I believed and followed the word of God.

I start walking back to Hill Top – my nan's house. As I'm walking, I'm still angry and confused, muttering negativity under my breath. As I arrive at the top of the street which leads to my nans, I'm walking down, but walking only on the kerb, which had a different shade to the rest of the pavement foot path. I guess boredom had settled in. As I'm walking, trying to balance on the kerb only, I fall off and almost fall to the ground and twist my ankle. Now I'm even more angry, firstly got no money, this faith business isn't working for me and now I almost died – in the heat of my emotion, I went from almost twisting my ankle, to almost dying now, it was only right.

As I catch my balance and look down, at the side of the kerb is a £10 note. I can't say 100%, but I'm 99.99% sure that the money was not there when I walking to the shop, I would have seen that! Had someone dropped it on the floor in between the time when I had walked past this area and was walking back? Was it supernaturally put there? I don't know, but one thing I do know is that what I asked God for was exactly what I got, not a penny more, not a penny less. I had learned something that would stick with me for the rest of my life:

"God may not answer you in the way you expect Him to, but He WILL answer!"

This gave me huge confidence, but I wanted to see more, I wanted to exercise more faith and see what else God would do.

"I wanted to exercise my faith the same way someone goes to the gym and exercises with weights, I would start small and build up."

At this stage Max, Aiden and I would go church every day. Monday night we would go the Bethel – Small Heath, Tuesday would be Bethel – Gibson Road, Wednesday night would be my church West Bromwich, Thursday – Gibson Road, and Friday, Gibson Road again for Bible class led by Elder Maclean, who was like a walking talking Bible, this man he knew the word and could bring it alive and make it so exciting. We all loved Friday nights and would often be the first ones there to help set out the tables and chairs. None of us were driving at the time, so we travelled by bus everywhere to get there and back home. There were a lot of nights I would get back just before midnight because the buses in my area were so infrequent, but I didn't care, I just wanted to be in church.

On one occasion, I went to Gibson Road on a Tuesday night, I can't remember why, but I was there by myself, Aiden and Max couldn't make it that day. I only had money for my bus fare to get me to and then from church. But now I want to exercise more faith, it's offering time, but the only money that I have is my bus fare. I prayed just like I did when I had previously gone to the cash point when I knew I had no money in there. I give my money, now I have no money to get home, this would now be God's responsibility to make a way and get me home. This time, no matter what I see, I wouldn't let my faith waver or more or complain as I did last time.

Church finishes, people are greeting everyone, I go around greeting as many people as I can, in my mind, God will use someone to offer me a lift. People start leaving now, I don't know if it was the devil or my own negative thoughts, but a thought comes into mind saying, "You better start preparing to walk from Handsworth to Hill Top."

As I start walking to the exit, I see a man who looks like my dad, but it can't be, because my dad works in London from Sunday night and returns home on a Friday evening, in fact at this age, he spent a lot of time out of the country in Ireland and USA for work, so it can't possibly be him. I walk closer to this man and it is my dad, I ask him why he is back from London and why is he at midweek church, he never went church unless it was Christmas or Easter, much less as midweek service. He explained he had to do something or meet someone on this particular day and had to be back, but most importantly, he would be the answer to my prayer. This helped strengthen my faith even more and built up my trust in God, something that I would need later on in life.

Back in school, I would go on to take my GCSE exams and complete course works for specific subjects. On results day, I walk down from Hill Top to see how I got on. Just as was the case with my German coursework, my RE teacher also thought I wouldn't amount to anything academically, she gave me a predicted grade of a 'U', the normal grades were 'A' to 'F', but she felt I couldn't even do that and again, I can't blame her based on my behaviour and output during the lesson. What she didn't know was that I was Christian who knew the Bible very well, again I can't blame her based on my behaviour. So when I get to open my results and I got an 'A' grade, she was shocked, she even came over to me to apologise for the prediction she gave me. I was quoting Bible scriptures in my exam like a teenager quotes the lyrics from their famous song. I could only succeed.

In total, I got 1 'A' grade, 4 'B' grades and 3 'C' grades. So based on the financial incentive given to me by my dad and Daddy Fletcher, I made a tidy sum money. That summer we would go to Cheshire Oaks shopping centre where I would spend my winnings. Now I'm seeing results and benefits in my spiritual life and natural life – life is good!

The next year, I started 6th Form, a lot of people had left Menzies to go to college for higher education. A popular choice for a lot of people was Sutton

Coldfield College, it had a reputation amongst all the young people as the place to be for the social environment. From the boys' perspective, it had a lot of attractive girls, so there was a strong allure. At Menzies, it had the total opposite reputation and experience. I stayed because it was what I needed rather than what I wanted.

"Sometimes in life, you have to make decisions based on what you need, rather than what you want – maturity required."

The subjects I chose were Business Studies (Double Award), Economics and English Literature. Amo was in all my classes, this would continue going into university. Liam stayed at 6th form too but studied different subjects. Though Max and Aiden left the year before to go to college, they would return to visit infrequently, especially as they lived locally. Ashton went to a different High school, Churchfields, but he and a few of his friends would transfer over to our school for 6th form.

I remember hating 6th form with a passion, particularly the Economics class. I wanted to study the subject and from the outset it looked interested, but I struggled to make sense of the subject. I tried hard with the initial subjects, when I didn't do so well, I just stopped trying. I would sit in the class, staring out the window literally counting down the time in each lesson and the days before I could leave 6th form.

At church, I was still going through my usual seasons of a fluctuating mentality. Max, Aiden and I were still going to church every day, it had been like this for some time. Aiden and I got closer as friends and would talk and confide in each other about how we were feeling as young teenagers. Max was doing good and didn't seem to be struggling at all. We all tried sticking together after school and on weekends. We would go to the local pub and play pool very often, for Aiden and I it was a distraction from our hormones at times when we were not in church.

Aiden's family would then move from Hill Top to Handsworth Wood, at the time it felt like losing a brother, but it wouldn't be long before Aiden started driving, his first car was a black 'S' reg Fiat Punto. Now that Aiden was driving, we could go anywhere we wanted and even get to church without catching buses. At this time, Max and I were taking our driving lessons.

As me and Aiden were talking more and confiding in each other, I could see that he was struggling with church. In those days, we called it backsliding, that's when someone would leave church and go back to 'The world' for a life of sin. Having a car at a young age came with a lot of temptation and opportunities.

I remember one time Max and I were at my grandparent's house in West Bromwich, we decided to go to the shop. As we walk closer, it looks like Aiden's there outside the shop, we're both excited to see him and call out to him and wave to signal him. As we get closer, he's blasting out music from his car and he's with other people, two girls and another guy, who grew up in Hill Top. Everyone looks and feels awkward, as we get closer, we all just give each other a nod of acknowledgement and no words are exchanged. Max and I go into the shop, get what we need and walk back to my grandparents' house.

Sometime later, Aiden and I speak, I ask him how he's doing and what's happening. He tells me he's struggling because of women and temptation and can't be dealing with fake people who act like nothing bothers them, they too don't struggle and have a false image of perfection. What could I say, he already knew that I felt the same way about girls and temptation, and he was right about people acting like they were perfect. There was no one in church, especially around our age that was transparent to help young men and say, "I know how you're feeling and what your experiencing, I've been there, but let me show you and teach how to get through this." So Aiden, like a lot of young people, just left because they couldn't maintain this standard of living; going church five days a week and playing pool, didn't stop you feeling horny and girls tempting you. Aiden and I would still remain friends because we understood each other, but for the next couple of years, we wouldn't be as close as we were now on different paths.

Back at 6th form, I would still hate every moment, but now that I'm older, my hormones are raging! The same girl who gave me a brief 'shine' back in year 8, is also at 6th form, only now her body is fully developed, and she is only too happy to show it off in the summer with miniskirts and skimpy tops. Many days after school, it would be Noah, her and I walking back from school. At this point, I just can't help myself, I feel like I'm going to explode with all my natural God given hormones. I was struggling badly.

Chapter Reflections

- *Do you have things in your life that you use as justification to do whatever you want? There are people out there who have the same experiences as you, who have chosen not to allow the past to determine their decisions, why can't this be you?*
- *Have you ever tested/exercised your faith in God?*

Chapter 8
From Religion to Relationship

I would continue to struggle to the point where subconsciously I believed that this was just how things are. One Sunday, I go to church for evening service, by this time, my church had stopped renting and now had a mortgage on their own building in Tipton. One of the women on the choir would go into the pulpit to speak, her name was Sharon, she would also play an important role in my journey later on. She starts speaking about this '40 minutes for 40 days' with God. Every day, you dedicate 40 minutes of praying, reading, worshiping consistently for 40 days. When I hear this, I just know this is for me, at this stage in my life I am desperate and will try anything. It was difficult at the start for the first days. I would read and pray, look at the time and see that I had something like 35 minutes left. But as the days went by and I stuck to it, it became easier and easier. Church had taught me how to be religious and how to fast and pray, but now I would learn how to have a relationship with God. I would learn to know His voice and how to actually build a real relationship just like you would with a regular human being.

    I still felt horny, but not as much, the more time I spent with God, the more my sexual appetite decreased. My appetite was now for God. I would now come home from 6th form and pray and read, I would wash my mind by reading the word. All the big breasts and big bottoms that I had seen that day, would be washed from my mind and my mind would be renewed.

    It was around this time, where I really started studying about the things of God, there was a library of books at Hill Top and at home and I would go through them one by one, increasing in knowledge, which in turn helped me with my relationship with God. My prayers changed from a one-way conversation full of requests, now to a two-way conversation. I would pray and ask God how He was, how He was feeling and how His day was going, I became very sensitive to His voice. One time I was at home studying a book at the foot of my bed on the floor, as God and I are in mid conversation, I hear Him laugh, immediately I stop. I couldn't fathom that God could laugh or even have a sense of humour. I was never taught things like this at church.

During this period, I wasn't perfect, I still made mistakes, but they were much fewer than before. Around this time, my grandparents (Mom's side) decide that they want to move to Florida to live permanently, Helen too was looking to join them. That summer, my dad, mom, sister, grandparents, Helen and I go to Florida to help get furniture for the houses my grandparents and Helen have just purchased.

This was a real test for me spiritually, especially being in Florida when women where hotpants and skimpy clothes. I remember when I first get there that my hormones are raging, it felt like being exposed to real life porn. After a day or so, my mind calms down, I had brought my study books with me and maintained everything that I had learned back home. I couldn't believe it, I was fine.

"I realised for the first time that I have a choice and don't have to be a slave to my urges – if I decided."

The holiday felt like the film Groundhog Day, we got up every day, ate breakfast, went furniture shopping, went to McDonalds, then home, sleep and repeat. It wasn't a normal holiday, but I had my books and newfound relationship to occupy my time.

One day, we go to this to check out some furniture, some of the staff look at us but don't greet us or come to assist us. There was an Indian man working that day, his name was Jaggy. He was really polite and helpful. He comes over to see how he can help, you can only imagine the look on his face when he is told that we need to fill two empty houses, everything from beds and sofas to tables and cabinets. Tens of thousands of dollars were put down that day, the other staff who had previously ignored us, now all of sudden wanted to come over and help us – but it was too late, and they were promptly dismissed.

"Be careful how you treat people, you never know who they are and what they can do for you – manners will take you far in life!"

When we get to the UK after Florida, I'm still maintaining my new relationship, everything seems okay. Shortly after I have my theory test with the DVLA. The test station was in Dudley, on the day I only had money to catch the bus there but no money to get back, poor planning on my side. But I didn't care, because if I passed, I wouldn't mind walking back to Hill Top. I took the test, I passed the hazard perception, I found that easy, but I fail the questions, there were 35 and you had to get at least 30 to pass, I get 29 and I'm fuming with myself and God. I thought being a Christian with this new relationship meant that I wouldn't suffer or go through hard times, I would learn that this wasn't the case and would have plenty of time to let this new found revelation sink in as I walked 7.5 miles back to my Nan's which took around three hours.

Before I would retake the test, I had a dream, me and these dreams! In the dream, I take the hazard perception test as before, but with the 35 questions, as I am looking at the multiple-choice questions, the hand of an angel or God becomes visible to me and it's showing me the answer. I wake up, in my head this means God is going to help me and give me the answers. I go to the test centre excited and confident; God is with me! I do the hazard perception test as before and I know in my mind I have passed that as it's easy for me. I now start on the 35 questions, I blitz through the questions answering all the ones that I definitely 100% percent know the answer to and then come back to the ones where I'm not quite sure. I tally up all the answers that I know I have right, it's 29, I just need one more answer and I have passed. It was a timed exam and I had about 15 minutes left. I just stare at the screen, waiting for a hand to appear just like in my dream, to show me the answer. I get down to the final minutes, but nothing has happened, God has to show up, he has already proved himself recently with the cashpoint and ten-pound note and at church when my dad randomly turned up – I believe God! The test invigilator is walking around the room as there are other people taking the test, he sees me slumped backed in my chair just staring at the screen, he must have thought there was something wrong with me. He comes over and looks at my screen, it's currently on one of the questions that I don't know the answer to. As he stands behind me, he reaches his arm over my shoulder and points with his hand to the answer to the question, just like in my dream, but this time it's not a spiritual hand, it's a physical hand. As soon as he shows me the answer, I end the test and click out. I go for my results, I passed with 30/35! I'm overjoyed and remember what I learned before:

"God doesn't always answer your prayers in the way you want, but He WILL answer!"

Shortly after, I take my actual driving test and pass first time with seven minors – prefect imperfection! My parents buy me my first car, it's a blue Vauxhall Corsa. I am free and on the road; the world is my oyster. I loved having my own car and independence. Shortly after, I turn 18 and enter into my last year of 6th form. Everyone starts attending open days at different universities to help decide where to attend. Me, Amo and another guy from 6th form travel to Coventry university in my car. We all hate it; we want a balance where we can get good education and also enjoy a good social life.

I wanted to go to Main Birmingham university or Aston University to study Business Economics, they both give conditional offers, where I would have to get certain grades to be accepted.

Church is going well and despite having a car, there's not a lot of temptation, most of my time is still spent going to church every day as it was before to occupy my time. My personal relationship with God is getting better and better and I'm still working on my gift – preaching.

Towards the end of the year, my mom would fall pregnant with my brother Christian, which was a shock to everyone as she was in her 40s.

The rest of that year seemed to go pretty quickly with most things in my life remaining constant. The next year in 2004, my bother would be born in July, and I would also get my 6th form results. I wouldn't get the results I wanted, so had to go to BCU – Birmingham City University based in Perry Barr. It would be Amo, Ashton and I that would travel there together, then shortly we would make acquaintance with Ricky who was up from London, the four of us would spend a lot of time together. I enjoyed university in the half of the first year, everything was new and excited, I was meeting new people and having good success academically, plus the first year never counted to your overall grading after the three years, you just needed to pass each subject with a minimum 40%, so there wasn't any real pressure. This contributed to our decision to spend most of our time playing football games on the PlayStation.

Aiden and I were still friends, but around this time we would start to spend a lot more time together. He had been going to the gym for a while and got, what we used to call 'hench', meaning muscular. As I needed something else to occupy my time when I wasn't at church, I would start to join him. Plus at this time, like with all young boys at this time in their life, I became conscious and more aware of my body, couple that with the fact that girls liked guys with muscles, this gave me all the motivation that I needed.

At this stage in my life, things were good, there were new things like university and gym that gave levels of excitement to my life, and I was coping well at church with my urges. But all this was about to change and my life as well as many others would be forever changed and impacted…

Chapter Reflections

- *Have you ever prayed for God to answer your prayers in a certain way, but he answers in a different way that blows your mind?*
- *What are some of your greatest moments spiritually?*
- *What things have you put in place in an effort to get closer to God and develop your relationship with Him?*

Chapter 9
My Worst LCI... But '... It's Not Like Anyone Died'

Later that year in 2004, my brother Christian was born in July. My mom had a good relationship with Dr Cawley, the preacher from Canada, the same one that came over every year for the revival at All Saints church in Wolverhampton and also the one that preached when my aunty Sally came back to church.

There was a time in Canada, where my mom, Helen and Mommy Fletcher had gone to a church convention. At the airport, Dr Cawley was there and the seating was organised in way where two people could sit together and the other would sit next to Dr Cawley – which nobody wanted. At this point, all they knew was that he was a powerful preacher who was well known in Canada and the UK. He was practically famous in church circles; what would you talk about for an 8-hour flight? Would you even talk, or just sleep part way and pretend that you're sleeping for the rest of the way?

The tickets are issued and my mom pulls the short straw, Mommy Fletcher and Helen are laughing between themselves. On the plane, once it takes off and reached the desired altitude, my mom and Dr Cawley begin to speak, much to her surprise, she can see that he is down to earth 'real guy' and really easy to talk to. Everyone had this perception, that because he was a powerful preacher, that he had no sense of humour or personality. From that point, Dr Cawley as well as a few of mentees became close friends to the family. This was to the point, that when it came time to choose godparents for Christian, Dr Cawley was chosen, as well as other high-profile people in Bethel. All of my brother's godparents were spiritual giants in the kingdom of God, plus my mom named my brother 'Christian', this child is obviously destined for greatness...

At this stage in my life, I was and was told that I was very naïve in terms of my perception in life and particularly people's behaviour. It's like I thought certain people were perfect and never struggled, especially when there was no evidence to suggest otherwise.

I remember one of my friends asking me about my dad, he was still working away from home Monday to Fridays, this would have been the seventh year in the row. Because it had been so long, it just felt normal. My friend asked me, "What does your dad do, man?" I asked what they meant. "He's away from home ALLL week, he must get crazy horny, plus he's got money and a good career profile. Don't you think he cheats? He must do…" When I heard that, I paused, I had never ever thought about that, I had never thought of my dad as a normal man with a sex drive, he was just my dad who was strict, ambitious and hardworking. Plus in my environment, I didn't know anyone that had cheated in their relationship, I only saw these things on television soaps and dramas. I responded back, "Nahhhh, my dad's not like that."

My friend looked at me with a stare to say, "You're so naïve."

The next year in 2005 would be my second year at university, but my first year in terms of results that count and contribute to my overall grade. In 2005, I'm still the same old naïve church boy, who has never drank alcohol, smoked or lost his virginity and I was going to maintain this in my head.

One day, I'm at Aiden's house, I think it was a Friday night, Noah was there and we were playing a football game on the PlayStation. It was getting late, I don't know why but I remember it was 11:55pm. I get a random phone call from my dad, he didn't really call me much and especially not that late. So of course, I'm thinking someone had died or there's some bad news.

He asks if I can meet him in West Bromwich town centre outside McDonalds ASAP, I was like, "Errm… okay." It sounded serious, but I could tell this would need to be a face-to-face conversation, so I don't even ask him to explain there and then. My car was at my Nan's house, Aiden had picked Noah and I up earlier that day, so all three of went down to West Bromwich. As we arrive, my dad is sitting in his car outside McDonalds in the dark, the whole area was quiet and secluded. Aiden parks his car about 100 metres away from my dad's car, then I get out walk over, racking my brains, trying to figure out what was happening.

When I get int the car and close the door. My dad sort of just jumped right into the conversation. As he's talking, he is facing forward with no eye contact, but I look at him at the start. He states that he and my mom are breaking up… I then join him and stare out the window in front me. He continues, he says that he has been cheating and got another child, a daughter, who is the same age as my brother Christian. This was a lot to take in, especially with me being so naïve and having Disney film perspective on life. I have no words and don't know what to do, I just freeze. I don't know why I did, but I ask him if he's okay and where he would be staying, he responds and says he will go to a hotel. I remember saying that I wanted to see my half-sister, after all, she is an innocent party in this mess. My dad says he will arrange it.

What I didn't know at that time, was that the only reason my dad was telling me was because he got caught and my mom found out, so in my mind he was only being open because 'the cat was out of the bag'.

As I leave and go back to Aiden's car, obviously they are keen to know what he said, we're all like brothers, so I tell them, after all my dad is leaving anyway, it's just a matter of time before everyone else finds out anyway. They are as shocked as me and have no words, my only thought now is to get home to my mom and see how she is. Once Aiden drops me to my car, I quickly jump in and race home. As I'm driving home, tears start flowing, I'm crying because I'm in shock, my family has now broken and I'm mostly hurting thinking about how this impacts Mom.

As I get closer to home, I try to compose myself. I'm now outside my house and I am dreading going inside. I wipe the tears off my face, I don't want my mom to see that I've been crying. As I walk upstairs and go into the bedroom, I can't remember if my mom was already crying or if she started when I told her that my dad had told me what's happening. My mom starts apologising and saying he shouldn't have done that without speaking to her first. She starts crying more and keeps apologising for the current situation, I don't know what to do or what to say. All I know is that I hate my dad for what he did to this family and especially to my mom. All I that was running through my mind was "What kind of man does this to his wife and children?", "You're meant to be the protector, not the one inflicting hurt and pain", "All my life, you've been so strict with me and you've been living a lie, a double life, what a hypocrite!"

I hold my mom as she cries on my shoulder, I can't imagine how she's feeling and what she's going through, especially as I had never had a proper relationship and experienced heart break. With my church boy, naïve-to-life mentally, I try to help and say something like, "I know it's bad right now and that you're in pain, but all things work together for Good and God will bring purpose out of your pain. One day, you will show your scars and help others who will go through what God is going to bring you through."

When I was five years old and went to the emergency room after I went through the glass door and got the scar on my arm; my mom said that one of the worst things is to watch someone you love be in pain and not be able to do anything about it... now we had come full circle and switched roles. This was my worst life changing incident that I had ever experienced to this day. The next day, which would have been a Saturday, I get up and check up on my mom, then tell her I'm going out for a bit. As I'm out and begin to reflect on the night before, I break down and burst into tears. I was hurt and angry. I was angry because my dad caused all this mess, but then would return to London for work, leaving my mom to deal with everything. Later, it was my mom that had to deal with the embarrassment and shame, whilst informing family and close friends, whilst my dad dealt with zero consequences. I wanted him to pay for what he did to us.

My dad was still close with Ashton's parents and so was my mom. One time, my mom was at their house to pass by and after keeping everything to herself for over a year, just broke down and confided in them. Colin, Ashton's dad was my dad's cousin, but was sympathetic to my mom and not happy with my dad, as anyone would be. Sadie, Ashton's mom, who is a friend that has your back all the way, just saw red and at the very least had to speak to my dad and give him a piece of her mind. When she finally meets with my dad and verbally lays into him, part way through her rant, he interrupts and says, "... It's not like anyone died." When Sadie hears this, she blows her top and goes into another gear in her rant. When I heard what my dad had said, any respect that I previously had left, if there was any, immediately disappeared. It felt like he wasn't even sorry and showed no remorse. During this time, anything negative that my dad said or did was multiplied in my head. If he stole £5, in my head he stole £5,000, from this point on, he could do no right.

"Be careful what you say and do, your words and actions have consequences that can last for the rest of your life, worst still, other people's lives."

My feelings towards my dad were confusing, when he wasn't there, I hated him, but when he was around or when I saw him, I had this mercy and soft spot, just like that night when we spoke outside McDonalds, and I asked if he was okay.

Sometime later that year, I would meet my half-sister for the first time and as a by-product, her mother. As my dad and I wait for them to show up the chosen location, in my head I'm expecting some kind of stunning super model. Afterall, if you're going to destroy your family and cause life lasting consequences, at least make sure it's worth it – in this context. They come in. I look at the woman before I look at my sister… I can't believe my dad has put everything on the line for this woman. As a 19-year guy, at his sexual peak in terms of appetite, I don't see any outstanding features or anything noteworthy.

It was around this time that I find out that this woman and my half-sister who were living outside of London, had been up to West Bromwich and met my dad's mom and other members of my dad's family, I was so disappointed, hurt and felt betrayed by them all! I was fuming! It wasn't until I got older that I realised that it wasn't their responsibility to reveal anything and they in fact were put into a very awkward position. It was a position that I would come to know myself down the line with my dad.

My parents had decided to tell my sister the news, this time they would both be present, after my dad jumping the gun with me, this time my mom wanted to make sure it was done properly – if there is a 'proper' way to tell a 7-year-old something like this. We were all at home, it was left to my dad to break the news, it was the least he could do and the only responsibility he took on from my perspective at the time. When my sister was seven years old, she was very much a daddy's girl and my dad would often spoil her with gifts and the things she wanted. He would quite happily sit down on a Saturday morning and watch her kiddies' programmes, no problem. But when I wanted to watch wrestling, it just wasn't allowed, so my dad had a soft spot for my sister. All this would change with this one conversation, my sister starts crying instantly and my mom, trying to be positive, says it will be okay, everything will be fine. I sit there staring at my dad in the corner of my eye, but hey… "it's not like anyone died," right?

With all this happening, it felt too much for my naïve little mind. It almost felt like my whole life was a lie, it was crazy. Simultaneously, I was struggling with church and sexual urges, before I had these standards and rules that I wouldn't break, but now all that had gone out the window, I see things differently now. It's like I didn't care about anything anymore. In my body, I wanted to leave church and really explore life, but in my spirit, I was hanging on by a thread for dear life and I had no one in church to talk to either – I was alone. Again, there were no role models that would stand up and say, "I know how you must be feeling right now as a young man with hormones, I've been there, let me show you how I got through this, walk in my footprints." On top of this, Aiden, one of my best friends, had already left church, at least I'd have a friend out there in the 'world'.

I remember going to church at this point and just crying, my head and emotions were all over the place and I was searching for a reason to stay in church. All my experiences and encounters that I had were now drowned out by the noise of my pain and my inability to do anything to help my mom and sister. For my brother, he would have a life never knowing what it's like having a father in the home – I know reading this you may think, "well that's the same for most children, that just means that we as a society, have become desensitised to fatherlessness and accepted it as the norm. For me at that the time, it was alien."

I was still going to Friday night Bible class at Gibson Road at this point. On one particular Friday, it was just me and Noah that went. This would be the day that I would make the decision to leave church and 'backslide'. After Bible class, I decide to go to Broad Street in Birmingham city centre where all the clubs are, I wanted to see what all the fuss was about and see how other people lived. As I'm driving on Broad Street, there's traffic and cars are slowly moving forward. Whilst in traffic, Noah and I were taking in the views of the atmosphere and the women – this is all new to us. As I'm taking in all the views and I look at the cars going in the opposite direction, I see Aiden's black Fiat Punto, I look to the driver and see Aiden and he then sees me.

He gives me a look of shock with his eyes that asks, "what the hell are you doing here?" I put my hands up and shrug my shoulders to say 'Dunno', then we both smile and nod our heads. From that day, we were inseparable, two church boys out in the world on an adventure together.

Not too long after this, I had arranged to see my dad in London. I had decided to make a trip out of it, Noah and Aiden joined me and we got a hotel. After seeing my dad, Aiden arranged a 'flex' through a friend in London. We went to his friend's house and waited for these girls to show up, but it never happened. Tired and frustrated, we drive from one side of London to the other. When we get back to the hotel, it's about 4am, Noah and Aiden decide to get some alcohol. When we all get back from the shop with a bottle of Southern Comfort and a chaser, they ask if I wanted any. I had never drunk before and to be honest, it wasn't something that really interested me. But the new me, was oh too happy to try now. I remember getting drunk, using the hair dryer in the hotel despite my hair being dry and sorting out the packet of Skittles by putting all the colours together on the table. It was my first time with alcohol, and I loved how it made me feel, it made me forget about all problems… for a period.

When we get back to Birmingham, Aiden would introduce me to his flexes. Noah and I would call him the flex master, as he always had different girls and at the age, it was something that most guys wanted. I remember the first-time meeting one of Aiden's girlfriends, looking back I was initially shy at that time.

Aiden had gone to Sutton Coldfield college where there were lots of attractive girls, whereas I had stayed at Menzies where there weren't any girls to really engage with. Furthermore, my mentality was not to get emotionally involved with anyone, as I didn't see the point as it wouldn't end in marriage, so I was quite stand offish with girls and didn't believe that men and women could just be friends, whereas Aiden had the total opposite mindset to me. He had a few female friends and was very personable with women on an emotional level.

Aiden would continue to introduce me to his female friends on different occasions, it was almost like a training exercise for me to practice speaking to women. On one occasion, it was me Aiden and one of his friends, we were on the dual carriage between Perry Barr and Newtown in Birmingham. Aiden and his friend were smoking a cigarette, his friend out of courtesy goes to pass this cigarette to me but Aiden intercepts and lets his friend know that I don't smoke. But that was the old me, now I'm staring at the cigarette in the same way I stared at the bottle of Southern Comfort when I tried alcohol for the first time. All my defences and standards had dropped. Now I had become a smoker and it was long after this that I went from smoking cigarettes every day to smoking weed every day, even Aiden thought that was a step too far.

Next, I had decided to get a tattoo, again this wasn't something that I had ever considered, particularly as in Bethel, my church organisation, tattoos were seen as sinful. But all I knew was that I wanted one. This desire was intertwined with my low self-esteem, I had the scar on my arm from when I was five, but I also had two bullet like scars from my TB vaccinations from when I was around 8, my body never reacted to it and formed scars. So I wanted a tattoo that would cover these. At least I could wear T-shirts and people wouldn't see it. The only reason why I didn't get a tattoo on my forearm over my other scar, was because I wanted to hide my tattoo from 'Church people'.

So I book myself in for my tattoo at Selfridges in the Bull Ring in Birmingham City centre. That morning, I couldn't eat because I was so nervous, I didn't know what to expect. Aiden came with me for support, but he had to wait outside whilst I had the procedure. During the whole procedure, I look away and listen to music on my iPod to distract me from the pain. A few hours later and I have a tattoo, I didn't let anyone know that I was getting one except Aiden, so I had to let my mom know. Normally, this would have been a difficult situation, but with my new mindset, I just didn't care. I let my mom know, she doesn't say anything, but her silence was deafening. I wasn't considering how she felt and how my actions could further affect her mood negatively. So now, I drink regularly, I'm a smoker and now I have a tattoo, all in short space of time. There was only one thing left…

One of the Fridays, Aiden and I went with Noah to see his dad at his pub in West Bromwich, Fox & Dogs. His father was a co-owner. As we go into the pub, Noah speaks to Dad whilst Aiden and I just chilled. It was mainly an environment for older people in their 40s and 50s, but it quickly became a place where we would spend our Friday and Saturday nights. Eventually, it grew and grew until there were two rooms, one for the older people and then one for the younger people. It had a great atmosphere and attracted a lot of people.

One time, Noah and I were in Carters Green in West Bromwich, I didn't have a car that evening, so we jumped into a taxi, there was a girl who was going in the same direction, so she joined us. I started speaking to her and got her number. She was the one that first introduced me into smoking weed, she was a little older than me and was from West Bromwich, though I had never met her before. One time we meet and we're chilling in my car, one thing leads to another after smoking some weed. Every other sexual encounter I had been through, I was never ready or lacked understanding, this time would be different, the only thing standing in my way was my own nervousness. It felt like my inner being was rejecting this moment or God was giving me a chance not to cross over this LCI. In the end, nothing happened that night. But a few days later I was determined to crossover, it was like I was spiritually disabling any protection God had over my life to indulge. I meet the girl at her house and lose my virginity, I felt weird, different, the same as when I was 13 and had experienced oral sex for the first time.

I remember the next day, Aiden came to my Nan's house in Hilltop, and I told him that I lost my virginity, there was that same smile and nod of affirmation that I had received in the past, it was like I hungered for this from any source. Now I felt like a man, I felt like I was coming into my identity.

Now that I had lost my virginity, I literally changed into a completely different person who now drinks, smokes and has sex, I was unrecognisable in my character – something that people around me would tell me. It was almost like I had no conscience anymore. Whilst I could never blame my dad for the decisions that I made, his actions were definitely a contributing factor. That been said, if it wasn't my dad's actions, then something else would have triggered me.

"Hard times and adversity show a person who they really are."

It's easy to look at others and judge, but until you are exposed to certain experiences in life, you just don't know how you would react. Before all this happened, I would look at people who were imperfect and judge them in my mind, but once I had been through my own problems and I myself became imperfect, it caused me to look at people in a different way.

Chapter Reflections

- *Have you ever had things in your life that you were in denial about? Is so, what were they?*
- *What was the first thing that happened in your life that cause you to grow up instantly and see the world very differently?*
- *Have you ever reached 'rock bottom' in your life? When did it happen and how did you deal with it?*

Chapter 10
Life After Death

My dad once said, "It's not like anyone died," but nothing could be further from the truth, the person who I once was had died, now I'm this whole new person. The person who my sister was died and she had hatred in heart that needed to be treated with therapy. The person who my mom was had died as she was no longer a married woman, but rather a woman separated from her husband and as a whole, our family unit that once existed was now dead. Now everyone is trying to navigate through life after all these deaths.

I was continuing in my new lifestyle, which consisted of drinking all the time, smoking weed, being promiscuous and coming home at the early hours of the morning, if indeed I came back at all. This was life after death for me and it became my new normal.

Later that year, my aunty Amelia would marry Noah's dad. I don't remember much from that day, the only thing I remember is my parents sitting together, at this point, people had no idea what was happening, as in the general public outside of immediate family.

My dad was still working away in London but was staying with his mother when he came up. In the early days, when my mom first found out about the affair, she packed my dad's things in a suitcase and asked me to drop it off to him, which I did. A couple of days later, I was at my nan's house (my dad's mom) and I was told how my nan was telling people how I thought I was some big man, dropping my dad's suitcase off as though I made the decision. When I heard this, I start raging within myself, I remember thinking, *Why weren't you running your mouth like this when you were entertaining my dad's mistress sipping on tea in your house?* But rather than say anything, I just walked out the house without explaining or saying bye to anyone. From that day, I would never engage in anything except an amicable conversation with my nan ever again.

Since that day, any time I went round there was because I was forced to, or my mom pleaded with me. With my newfound mindset, I was not in the place to put myself in certain environments.

Anyway, during this time, my parents had spent time together to work on their marriage, at the wedding reception my mom asks if I would be okay with my dad coming home, I was drunk so I said yes, had I been sober, I would have said no. So when my dad moves back in, it's very weird. Since he last lived here, I have changed drastically and pretty much done whatever I wanted. Now when my dad moves back, he tried to pick up where he left off – being a strict father with rules and curfews. So as you can imagine, we clashed. He would give me curfews which I would eventually ignore, even though the car that I had come from my parents and they helped significantly with the upkeep. But in my mind, my dad owed me after everything he did. I remember one night, my dad gave me a curfew which I blatantly ignored, when I got home late at night, he confronted me and reminded me about the curfew, to which I replied, "I'm not the one that needs a curfew," and stared at him with a mixture of anger, pain and hurt. In my mind, he no longer has any authority. For the next four years, I would have a love-hate relationship with my dad.

Life at home was very weird, to add to the weirdness, every other weekend, my half-sister Lilly would come up and stay over, I honestly don't know how my mom did this, I wasn't even the wife and I felt uneasy. Then sometimes we would all go out as a 'family'. I remember one time being in West Bromwich Pizza Hut all together and Sadie and Colin walked in; you could see the awkwardness all over everyone's face. Then I remember the first time all of us went to Hill Top together... so awkward. The only person that benefited from these awkward encounters was my dad, no one else certainly did not. When Lilly would come, it would be regular, so eventually it became normal, but it wasn't long until the visits became more and more infrequent. I don't know the reason why and at the time I didn't care to ask, again, I had nothing against Lilly, she was an innocent child, but at that time, her very presence was a reminder of what had happened and I didn't know how to process or deal with my feelings. Everyone else was fine, no one else was saying anything negative or complaining, they just adjusted back to how things were, so it felt like and seemed like I was the only one with a problem.

Lilly's mom is white and didn't know how to deal with a black child's hair, but every time Lilly would stay with us, my mom would do Lilly's hair, moisturise and style it, apparently this infuriated Lilly's mom. One time when Lilly was down, she would have been around five years old at the time, my mom was about to do her hair and she said, "My mommy said you can't do my hair no more." Of course Lilly was a child and is only saying what she was told, but clearly there was an issue.

I watched my mom embrace Lilly for years like she was her own daughter. Calesha and I were a bit stand off-ish when Lilly came in the early days, but still polite, but my mom went the extra mile. To this day, they both still have a good relationship and still talk. The other day, Lilly had booked her driving test and didn't tell anyone, but she told my mom.

Bad situations and circumstances reveal who a person really is and the way my mom has handled this situation for almost 20 years completely blows my mind, her character is on another level. I was hurt by what my dad did and I wasn't the main person to deal with all the pain, suffering and embarrassment and it drove me to alcohol, drugs and madness, but my mom who felt a deeper pain has always remained steadfast in her faith and character. The situation with my parents would continue with them both working on the marriage, because of where my head was at, I was totally oblivious to how well things were going. It would be another 5 years before another major incident, within that time, things seemed to go back to how they were, honestly with everything that was happening at the time, my memory about those 5 years isn't so good, but there was some form or peace and consistency.

Around this time, I started my first job at the previously mentioned Showcase cinema in Dudley. Up until this point, I had been totally reliant on my parents financially. My role was that of an usher, I cleaned the cinemas after a viewing and also watched films to ensure that the quality was sufficient. I never took the job seriously, one because I had this self-entitled attitude, where even my dad had said the job wasn't for me to earn money but to get used to working with people, and two, I still had this 'I don't care about anything' attitude. I remember taking an hour and a half lunch break when I was only allowed 20 minutes because I wasn't happy about something. On another occasion, I just sat in the cinema and watched films while eating food. We had several managers and one overall general manager, but they didn't know how to deal with me, I was one of only three or four black people on the team and they all felt awkward addressing issues, particularly with black staff. To be fair, I can't blame them, when I first started, they hired me and one other black guy, when it was time for our first week's pay, the system had malfunctioned and not paid us properly. I wasn't too fussed, but he went crazy, called down a car full of friends, who were sitting outside ready to come in and rob the place. One of the managers on duty had locked himself in the office out of fear, while one of the other black members of staff tried to calm everything down. So to many of the managers, how young black men are portrayed on television is true. I would end spending four years at showcase until I was coming to the end of my post graduate master's degree course at university.

At this point in my life, I was constantly angry and emotionally confused about how I felt towards my dad. One day, it would be as though nothing had ever happened and on another day, it was like I was full of rage. Looking back, counselling was something that I definitely needed to help process my feelings and deal with everything.

The next couple of years flew past and was a continuation of me at university, working at the cinema and living the same life of drinking, smoking and partying. In the winter, I would get home between 4am and 6am and then sleep the whole day, sometimes I wouldn't even see daylight, it was constant darkness, which was symbolic of where I was in my life. I had a few different relationships during this time, but because of where my head was at, I wasn't able to treat the women right, especially with my anger and bad attitude, so although I was seeing people, I never connected on an emotional level, it was just purely physical, but that's how I liked it.

At this point, I wasn't in or going to church. There were times where I wanted to go back, but those desires would quickly vanish as the temptations from women and the worldly lifestyle would take my attention. I remember going church, being at the altar crying and making the decision in my head to come back to church, then I'd get home a woman would text me to meet up and I just couldn't resist. I would be at revival church meetings and the power of God moved in the service touching everyone including myself, but an hour after church I'd be in a car park smoking. I was becoming desensitised to God's voice and all consequences. I understood that if I were to die at that time that I would be going to hell… but I just didn't care. It was go hard or go back to church, so I chose to Go hard. This was my life up until 2008.

During this period, around 2006, there was an altercation at work. I had one manager that just didn't like me. I knew most of them never liked me, but they wouldn't be so open about it, but there was one, we'll call him Paul, he was oh too happy to make me know.

One night at work, there was a brand-new film out and the cinemas were totally full. Normally, it would take two ushers to clean a cinema, but now we needed four. After the next showing, I was left to clean the cinemas by myself, doing the work of four ushers. As I came out of one cinema getting ready to clean another, Paul comes out and in front of everyone starts telling me off, saying I'm taking too long and then asking me why my shirt was hanging out. I explained that I'm doing the work of four people, so I'm not going to be as quick as normal and the reason why my shirt was hanging out was because I was running round and cleaning. He decided that wasn't good enough and sent me home, as I walked to the staff room to get my stuff, he comes up to me and squares up like he's ready to fight, I don't know if he was trying to get a reaction out of me, but I never responded. Instead, I would write a letter of complaint. I researched on the company website and found out who the key contacts were in the UK and US, then with the help of family members, I wrote a formal letter of complaint. Weeks later, a man who was a HR rep from the Nottingham branch came down and met with me and my dad to get my version of events. Later everyone who was working that day got interviewed, it was like a full investigation which got the attention of all staff.

Rumours began to spread that Paul may lose his job. Other managers during this process stayed well clear of me. They realised I wasn't the type of black man to fight with my fists, but rather with my mind and intellect. I was only too happy to show them that some black people know how to handle themselves in a work environment and we are educated to know how to deal with things according to employment law. In the end, Paul had to apologise to me, the letter stated all the facts, I was doing the work of four ushers with no help, I was told my shirt was hanging out by a manager who was not himself dressed according to company standards and my hours had been reduced to the absolute minimum, which is a form of constructive dismissal. This scenario would prove to be useful to me in the future.

We're now in 2008, Barack Obama is in the running to become the 44th President of USA, the U.S. economy faced the worst financial crisis since the great depression and the most popular films included Dark Knight, Iron Man and Mama Mia. Life had pretty much been the same for the previous couple of years, the year before in 2007 I had my first lad's holiday. Originally, it was meant to be Ashton, Aiden, Noah and I, but Noah was unable to come. We got up to all kinds of crazy stuff, but what happened in Florida, stayed in Florida!

During the previous two years, I started to get close to one of my cousins Tasha, she was on my dad's side. When I was 10 years old, Charlotte and I went to Jamaica with Grandad Beckford for four weeks over the Christmas period. Tasha was on that same holiday too, but after the holiday, I never really saw her again. One of the nights when I was out at Fox & Dogs, I was outside the building chilling with people smoking a cigarette and Tasha drove by, she was both shocked and disturbed as she thought I was still in church. I explained that I'm going through a 'phase' in my life. She was a member of Restorer church, which was part of the Jabula organisation, on the worship team. She encouraged me to come back to church; at that time, apart from my own family, it was only Tasha and a woman called Donna C from my old church that actually took time to reach out to see how I was and encourage me to come back to church.

It's not what you do in the pulpit for 30 minutes once a week when everyone can see you, it's what you do for the rest of the time, when people can't see you.

I was grateful for this from both people, no one knew that they were helping me, but they did it anyway. One day, Tasha is speaking with me and somehow manages to convince me to come to her church. So I go, when I get there, I see familiar faces, one is Liam from Menzies. It was a nice day, but I had no intention of coming back to church. Shortly after this time, I joined Facebook for the first time. I get a message from one of the women from Tasha's church, we'll call her Naomi. She says it was nice to see me at her church and we begin to speak. We have good banter together and get on well. She says she'll come meet me at the cinema when I'm working. So the next time that I'm at work, she comes, just like she says. I didn't remember seeing her at the church, so apart from her pictures on Facebook, I didn't know what to expect, but when she arrives I'm pleased.

At this time and even going back to Menzies days, it was almost fashionable for someone to date a person with dual heritages or whatever the politically correct way to say it. It was as though they were more desirable and up until this point, I had never been with a woman with this ethnic background, so this made me more excited.

As soon as she came, I got one of my colleagues to cover me, whilst we went into an empty cinema to get more acquainted. We instantly hit it off and before long we were in an unofficial, unnamed relationship.

I was at university at the time, my dad had won the lottery the year before and got £44K along with 10 other winners. He said he would either get me a new car or would pay for my master's degree, I chose the master's degree and I was given the car for making the right decision. I got a mini cooper, black and yellow in colour, then my dad got me some brand-new rims. At this point in my relationship with my dad, things were pretty much back to normal.

So I would go to university, work at the cinema and date Naomi. Many times I would finish work and go to her flat, she had her own place and a 2-year-old daughter at the time, when I got there she would cook dinner for me – this was something new to me, it felt like playing house. Naomi was very chilled, she would invite and let my friends around her home and I would meet her friends too. This was the first time that I had some form of balance in a relationship, but I was still very much keeping my guard up emotionally. This relationship started towards the end of 2008 and continued into 2009 till around April, it was six months in total.

In the first quarter of 2009, Restorer church, where Naomi, Tasha and Liam attended, were having a retreat at a hotel. I was neither for nor against it, so decided to go, I was seeing Naomi at the time, but kept my distance during the weekend. They had an agenda for the whole weekend, morning, afternoon and evening sessions with speakers. Before one of the lunch time sessions, it was offering time and the Pastor's wife called me to bless the offering. After I blessed the offering, we stopped for a break before the next session. As I was walking back to my seat, a man stopped me and asked me, "How are you? How are you doing mentally, physically, emotionally, financially? What is the plan for your life?"

I was stunned by the questions and just replied, "I'm at university at the moment, but I'm not sure what I want to do after that."

The man responded, "No, you must have a plan for your life! Get a book and write down 10 points/goals for your wife, finances, single life, relationship with God and your children."

This was something that I needed to hear, when the conference was over, I did exactly what the man had said and made a full plan, that plan has been the foundation to my entire life to this day! And I still have the same book and I'm very much in contact with that man today.

Later that evening, after the last session of the day, I was walking back to my hotel room. As I was walking down the corridor heading for my room, a woman that I knew, she used to be a member of my old church and knew my family very well, stopped me and asked if she could speak to me. She invited me into her room and said there's things laid on her heart that she feels led to say to me. I know it's not easy when God tells you to say something to a person, you have no idea what it means, but you're hoping it makes sense to them.

She starts speaking, as she moves through the sentences, she begins to quote lines from the prophecy that was spoken over me 10 years ago in Canada! My eyes widen and my heart opens. I'm in shock, but at the same time I'm so happy, I had forgotten about this prophecy as I hadn't heard or seen anything for 10 years! But God hadn't forgotten, despite my current state.

"So is my word that goes out from my mouth: It will not return to me empty but will accomplish what I desire and achieve the purpose for which I sent it."
Isaiah 55:11 (NIV)

As I went back to my room, I was just blown away, how could this woman quote the same words from 10 years ago in another country – she wasn't there! She said, "You will do things and people won't understand, you will excel." This was enough to give me focus.

Not long after, I start looking for a job, as I would shortly be finishing my university course. I interview at this sales company based in Birmingham city centre opposite New Street station. The owner explains that I can make as much money as I want, the harder I work, the more money I can make. When I heard this, I was excited. This is what I have been taught all my life from my dad. I could see myself been motivated here as opposed to my current attitude working at the cinema.

The job was commission only, with no basic salary, but all I heard was I can make as much money as I want. The owner, Shelly, was part of an organisation called Cobra at the time, later renamed Appco. They were a sale solutions company that sold companies goods and services on their behalf. So instead of paying millions of pounds on billboards, they would pay us and we would be the 'walking-talking advert', they would pay us, only once we sold something, rather than spending lots of money on advertising with no guarantees on a return of investment. Appco did this in three ways, business to business sales, event marketing (at shopping centres and supermarkets, like the SKY TV stands you see) and door to door sales.

The company was an international company that had clients such as SKY TV, TalkTalk, HSBC, British Red Cross and UNICEF to name a few. You could either just do sales and make money or you could build a team and then take your team to open up your own office anywhere in the world. There were five stages to get to own your own company and you decided how fast you got promoted through each stage by your own work ethic and performance.

At stage 1, you are a FR (field representative), once you do a minimum of 12 sales in a seven day week or 'rang the bell' (hit your daily target) three days in a row, you got promoted to stage 2 (Leader). On average, one sale would pay around £35, as we were not employees but contracted, we had to sort out our own taxes.

To get from stage 2 to stage 3 (Crew Leader), you had get a minimum of three people on your team and get them to stage 2 with a minimum profit of £1400 in a week. This amount was the national average breakeven point for a business. At this point, you are demonstrating you can lead, train and develop people whilst also breaking even as a business. Once you started building a team, you had a team name.

To get from stage 3 to stage 4 (assistant Owner), you had to have a minimum of five people to stage 2 (leaders) and produce a profit of £2,500 two weeks in a row. Usually by the time you get to this stage, you have a couple of crew leaders on your time building their own empires.

Once you're at stage 4, you just keep earning over £2,500 and that money goes into a separate account, when you hit £15K, you take your team wherever you want to set up and run your own business, you run the daily meeting, take care of recruitment and deal with the clients. Before you would make £35 per sale and the owner would make £35 off your sale, but when you become an owner, you make money off everyone's sales.

The job was very demanding, you worked seven days a week, hours were from 7:30am to around 7/8pm, depending on when you got back from the place where you were selling. This office sold TalkTalk and you could be selling in Birmingham or Telford, Nottingham or Leicester, so the days were very long. The idea was to work hard until you're around 40/50 years old and retire.

My owner Shelly was just 22 years old when she reached ownership, she was living in a Birmingham city apartment where some of the footballers lived, in the garage you would see all the top sports cars, so the results spoke for themselves. There were other owners around the country in their early 20s banking £20K–£30K per week, meaning after expenses and paying themselves a wage, they were saving these amounts, it was a different world.

Everyone around me thought I was crazy; I was an educated man who was about to get his master's degree and was getting a job with no basic salary selling TalkTalk in Morrisons supermarkets. But I had just been reminded after 10 years, that I will do things that people won't understand, and that I would excel and overtake. In my mind, this is what the prophecy means! I'll get promoted like Joseph in the Bible and with my position (ownership), I'll be able to help the church and my family, my purpose was now registering in my head…

Chapter Reflections

- When things don't go your way, how do you act?
- What was your first job and what did it teach you?
- Have you ever done something in life where everyone thought you were crazy? What was it and how did you respond?

Chapter 11
Purpose Registered...?

So now it's May 2009 and I start this new job, which I believe is linked to my purpose, there's just one small problem... I can't sell! I meet my team leader, Jag, he's a great guy, so positive about everything and most important, he's a sale monster winning multiple awards in the organisation. Our office was in the TalkTalk events division across England, Scotland, Wales and Ireland. On average, each office had around 25 people and there were around 20 different offices. Some offices had 80 plus people and some had 10, numbers were always fluctuating because of the nature of the job.

The job itself entailed meeting at the office in the mornings, those who were leaders at stage 2 started at 7:30am, whilst others would start at 8am. The leaders would get more comprehensive training on just how to sell, but also how to lead people, as well as training and developing people to be as good as yourself, if not better. At 8am, the leaders would join everyone else in the main office where there would always be loud music pumping to help create an atmosphere. There would be 'pitch practising' where everyone would go through their sales pitch to perfect it, this gave leaders the chance to work with their new starters to get them as prepared as possible before they went out to sell.

The last part of the meeting entailed the owner running sales and mentality impacts to both teach people how to sell and also to prepare their minds as the job involved a lot of rejection, which most people were not used to.

When I go out with Jag for my first day, we are selling in Kidderminster Morrisons. Jag is on fire making multiple sales, but I just feel awkward approaching random people as they are leaving with their shopping, in my mind, I wouldn't stop, so why would they. That day, Jag hits his target and donates two sales, one to me and one to another new guy. I loved the idea of being an owner and running my own business, but I hated the "field", that's the name of the place you go to sell. That day, the field was Kidderminster for me.

When we practised in the office, it was one thing, but going into the field was completely different, now I was dealing with real people. Trying to stop someone as they are leaving the supermarket with a trolley full of food shopping, pitching them for 2–5 minutes and convincing them to switch phone and broadband provider and also hand me their bank card to process the sale – it seemed impossible to me.

Days go by and I'm really struggling to sell, I get so frustrated that I walk out and sulk in the car. Jag had a lot of patience with me, I know I wouldn't have if I was in his position. In my interview, we were both convinced that I would hit the ground running based on the confidence I showed.

After five days with no sales, Shelly has had enough, she calls me into the office and tells me I better ring the bell (hit my daily target of two sales) or she is letting me go. We were in Worcester shopping centre that day, all of a sudden, I found the motivation that I needed and I made it happen. I made a decision to succeed because there was no other choice. Because I believed that this job was linked to my prophecy, I was convinced that I was un-fireable, so I was a lot more relaxed because God had no choice but to ensure that I succeed. After this, I now knew how to sell, the obstacle would be my own mindset.

I was desperate to succeed and couldn't afford for anything or anyone to get in the way of God's plan for my life. So I immediately and abruptly ended things with Naomi, the manner that I did this was very cold, I would later have to apologise for my behaviour in terms of how I ended things, but I knew that I couldn't have any distractions.

Because of the crazy hours, my university work was suffering, but in my head I was thinking, *I'm going to become an owner soon, so I won't need a master's degree anyway.* So, I had already completed my certificate stage and diploma stage, but I would forfeit the dissertation for ownership as I didn't have time to do both.

So now I was all in with no distractions. At this point, Ashton had heard what I was doing, he was finishing university but also wanted to join. He came to the office and met Shelly and Jag and spent a lot of time there learning about the business with Shelly before actually starting. He would go on to become one of the first leaders on my team. At this point, my whole life was changing, I was back in church, no longer smoking, not seeing any girls and 100% focused. I didn't really see my family because I was working these crazy hours and when I was at home, I was sleeping because I was so tired. For the next three years, this would be my life, my friendship with Aiden became pretty much dormant in this period, there just wasn't time or space for anything but work.

The culture in this business was to talk about success and be successful. You always had to be positive, negativity was never allowed. You weren't allowed any excuses if you missed your target, it was just your fault or you "lost your attitude", meaning you stopped being positive and had a negative mindset and it affected your performance. Every day the men were suited and booted and the women dressed up to. It was always about making money, getting promoted to the next stage and being super confident, but this almost always turned into arrogance. When you travelled to the different offices around the countries, most people were so arrogant, and they were proud about it. This culture started to filter into me the more successful I got.

After doing reasonably well with sales, Shelly put her faith in me and sent me to Holland on a free trip to spend time with some of the owners there with some other people from other offices. This was an attempt for me to see how big the organisation was and to further inspire me, it worked. Prior to leaving, I was still just getting to grips with sales, but when I came back, I wanted build my own team.

In the office, there was a girl there called Kal, she was amazing at sales and rarely missed her sale target. Everyone would talk about how she would be the next person to get promoted to Stage 3 (Crew Leader), I was never thought of as my sales record was average at best. There were a few of us on stage 2 building our teams, no on in our office had ever seen anyone get promoted to stage 3, Jag my leader was there already, but we had never seen it done.

A few months later in September, after a lot of hard work, sweat and plenty of tears my team and I hit £1400 and I was promoted, me, the guy who wasn't the best at sales. To me, this helped prove to me that God was with me and given me favour. As soon as I hit stage 3 (Crew Leader), my team just snow balled into success, two people on my team themselves became Crew Leaders, which in turn promoted me to stage 4 (Assistant Owner), I was on cloud nine! During this period I won three competitions were I got to travel to Spain for an all expense trip in a 5 star hotel, Malaysia for the same and lastly to Portugal where I took my mom to show her why I work so hard and for her to see that it's bigger than just selling TalkTalk. We had league tables for the different crews in their respective divisions, my crew was finally and regularly number 1 for a period.

During this period, I began to change as a person, but I myself didn't see it. I was walking differently and talking differently, I had gone pass being confident to full blown arrogance. One time, Shelly gave me a dressing down and said, "Who the hell do you think you are?" Then she sarcastically mimicked me and said, "Oooh, look at me, I'm James Beckford, I'm a crew leader." That night, she told me not to let success go to my head. Around this same time, I had started to drift from God, before my relationship was strong because I needed God to help me and I needed His favour, but when I reached a level of success, it was like I totally forgot about God.

"Whatever it took for you to get to a certain level in life, you will need the same thing to help maintain what you have obtained."

I got to a stage where I totally forgot about God, my lifestyle was like scenes from the film Wolf of Wall Street – constant work, always looking for more money and the next promotion, drinking, women and other foolishness.

From a work standpoint, at this stage, being an Assistant Owner, all I had to do was keep doing what I was doing until my account gets to £15K, then I take my team and become an owner and become a millionaire, easy-peasy… or so I thought. Around November 2010, Appco had lost their partnership deal with the supermarkets that they had been selling in all this time. So my office went from event marketing selling TalkTalk to door-to-door sales in the winter right before it started snowing. At this point, I had 22 people on my team, this went straight down to eight or nine people, as many people didn't want to work outside in the cold when it's raining and snowing and have to learn a new product. Before, I could fly in my dreams and I was manifesting that into reality; now, I couldn't even fly in my dreams. I was devastated, it felt like all my hard work for the past 18 months was all for nothing and I had to start all over again. I definitely thought about quitting, but this was where my purpose was.

The whole office, or those that chose to stay had to go to Bristol for a full retrain and learn how to sell knocking on doors again, it was like starting all over again from the beginning. Half of the office would go to Bristol, including myself, then come back and train the rest. Around this time, Shelly's boyfriend who was also an owner, moved from his office in Nottingham to New York,

Appco was now expanding to USA. This was taking a toll on Shelly and her focus, so much so, that someone reported back to her managing owner, who in turn sent someone from London to co-manage the office. Eventually, Shelly would leave and the office would be run by Patrick from London and he hated my guts.

Although, I was far from the best salesperson, I always had the biggest team and therefore the closest to getting promoted to ownership. Patrick had moved from London with two of his guys from his team. One was a sales animal, but could never build a team due to, in my opinion, her people skills. So her team had a revolving door. The other was less than average and would eventually leave sales and become the administrator.

My spiritual life would step up a gear like never before. If Appco had a HR department, Patrick would have been fired. To build your team, when you performed well, the owner would reward you with new people to help you build your team. But just as I did when I first started building my team, I would PR (personally recruit), I would create my own adverts on Gumtree and then interview people myself, Shelly had taught me how to interview and present the concept of what we do. So I was still doing this, but when my people came in to interview, Patrick wouldn't tell me and would hire them for himself, he did this on multiple occasions to the point where after all the bullying, all the indirect verbal assaults in morning meetings in front of everyone, after all the talking behind my back to members of my own team, who would obviously come back and tell me, I just lost it and we got into a screaming match in front of everyone, to the point where another owner had to get involved. Eventually, his owner back in London called me and I was open with her and told her everything that he had been doing, long story short, he had to apologise and give back what he had taken. But his behaviour would continue.

It got so bad, I would get anxiety about going to work and I couldn't sleep at night. That's when I started my 4am prayer that went on for years. I got up early at 4am everyday out of desperation.

"You don't know God until you know you can't go one day without Him and you KNOW you need Him every step of the way, every hour and every minute!"

This 4am prayer would continue for a great while, my mom would go on to join me. Once we lost TalkTalk and went to door-to-door sales, the hours changed to 10am start, but I wouldn't get back to Hilltop until 11:55pm. At this stage, my grandparents had stopped fostering, so I just ended up living there as it was just easier, rather than going all the way back to Willenhall. I would living there for the next six years. During my time living here, I would also start praying at night with Mommy Fletcher, I was desperate and needed all the prayer and focus that I could get.

Because I lost most of my team, I was automatically demoted by default from an Assistant Owner to a Crew Leader, from stage 4 to stage 3. After about 18 months to two years, frustration started to settle in, especially as I was so close previously to running my own company, coupled with the fact that Shelly had left and now Peter, who blatantly hated me was in charge.

I would be in the field trying to sell, but failing, there would be many times where I had tears in my eyes from frustration. I remember I used to call my mom emotionally drained complaining about the situation, whilst she would try to encourage me to keep going. It was like the more I tried to sell, the harder things got and the more that I failed. I was in the place where I should have been, in the place of purpose, but purpose wasn't manifesting. To add to this, Patrick was ramping up his public verbal assaults, it was too much for me. He did everything he could to bully, intimidate and belittle me and make me look bad; I remember one day it go so bad that I had to walk out the building. At this time, the office was in Birmingham city centre, opposite where the old Primark used to be, I walked a short distance, found a bench and just sat there, asking myself what I was doing with my life. Anything that could be wrong was wrong. Everything was leading up to the crescendo of my upcoming rock bottom experience.

In those days, we got paid weekly, whatever you sold the week before, you would get the following week. Remember with this job, there's no basic salary, so no sales means no money. After three years of working at Appco, in 2012 I found myself in a position where performance was bad to the point where I didn't even have enough money to catch my usual bus and metro to work, as I had been doing for the past year.

As I was living at my nan's in Hill Top, every morning my mom would drop my brother and sister to Hill Top for school. Normally by this time, I would have left for work, but this day I had no money. I got up and showered like I was going to work, knowing full well that I didn't have the means to travel. I hear my mom at the front door, so I run into the downstairs toilet. Normally, my mom would stay for five minutes and then leave for work. For some reason, on this day she's here longer than normal, but I decide to wait for her to leave before I come out – I can't deal with the embarrassment and all the questions, I'm meant to be on my way to running my own company, I'm that arrogant guy that's got it altogether.

Minutes are going by and she's still there, I must have been in the toilet for over 30 minutes at this point. It got to the point where I just couldn't hide anymore, because I had been hiding in the toilet silently, my mom assumed that I wasn't there, so when she hears the door open and realises that I'm there instead of work, she's understandably confused. She's sitting at the dining table and she calls me over… "Why are you here and how come you're not work?" I didn't know what to say, if I could have thought of a good lie, I would have told her. Instead, I decide to tell her the truth, as I begin to speak and explain that I don't have any money to get to work, tears begin to fall from my eyes, I can't even finish my sentence and I completely break down. I'm embarrassed, ashamed and humbled all at the same time. I had gone from almost running my own business, having the best sales team in my division, travelling the world after winning sales competitions, all the way down to rock bottom, where I'm hiding in the toilet because I don't have two pennies to rub together.

I thank God for my mom, she never agreed with me doing a job with no basic salary and this was the perfect time for a 'I told you' speech or to kick me when I was down. But instead, she comforted me, encouraged me and gave me money; me, a big 27-year-old man, bus money – it sounds so pathetic and that's exactly how I felt, I had never felt so low before.

> *"It's difficult to take, when you're doing everything right and everything you can and giving 100%, only for things not to improve and even get worse; especially when it feels like God is just watching and could easily help…"*

I was looking at my situation and thinking, work hard – check! Fast and pray to God – check! Work even harder – check! So why is nothing changing? Where is God?

One day, I was working in Darlaston, by the big Tescos, my aunty Sally was living in the area at the time. It was a Saturday and things were just the same, I was moving nowhere fast, Patrick was still being Patrick and my sales performance was still poor. As I was knocking on doors, trying to sell, it started to rain, it was one of those moments where you begin to notice all the details in your environment, you see every rain drop, you feel the direction of where the wind is blowing, you notice stones on the floor. I felt like I was just disconnecting from everything that should be important at the time. I pick up the phone and call my mom and ask her to pick me up, in that moment I just quit and threw in the towel. Thoughts of purpose and prophecies were not factored into my decision, it was purely based on how I felt at that time.

"Don't make long term decisions based on short term emotions."

To this day, this was one of my biggest regrets in life. I would never know what could have happened, especially to know if this was what was the means by which everything that was prophesied over my life would come through. Did I mess up God's plan for my life? Had I walked away from the very thing that God was using to bless me? That season, I prayed to God and said, "God, in future, when you're working on me and using situations in my life to refine me; no matter how much I ask, no matter how much I beg, moan or complain, NEVER let me out until the process is complete." Again, it's better to be uncomfortable and in God's will, then to be comfortable and out of His will.

Chapter Reflections

- *How have you handled success in the past?*
- *Have you ever had a time where you have worked hard for something over a long period of time, only to see it all fail and come to nothing? How did you respond?*
- *Do you have decisions in your life that you regret and that would have changed the trajectory of your life?*

Chapter 12
How Did You Get Here? Nobody's Supposed to Be Here

I had left Appco in the summer of 2012, 18 months prior I had got into a relationship with a girl on my team. Again, at this time, I still wasn't interested in a proper relationship, the closest that I had come to a relationship was with Naomi, but even then I was in full control of my emotions and very much had my guard up. Jazmine was a girl that had been on my team for well over a year, but I never looked at her in 'that' way, one because at that time I was well on my way to my next promotion, which would have been stage 4 – Assistant Owner and two, because it was frowned upon to be involved with someone on your team as things almost always ended badly and impacted on people's performance.

When Jazmine first starts, I help to train her, we were at Smethwick ASDA at the time, we got on well and both performed well too. For a period of time, after work, Ashton and I would drop her home as she lived on the way and even speak with some of the guys in her family, it was just a good working relationship. Besides, she had a boyfriend who she had been with for years, he even came to one of our awards ceremonies, he was a nice guy, although he lived in London, so they didn't see each other often.

After Appco lost the supermarkets and most of my team quit, Jazmine was one of the few that stayed, she never came to Bristol for the big retrain, in terms of learning the new products and how to sell door-to-door, so when I got back, I was one of the people that would with be with her and show her how to sell. In the field, going from door to door, we had a good time on our first week out, as I spent a few days with her, I started to like her as a person, but nothing more than that. After all, I had just lost over 50% of my team and I had no time for any distractions.

One night, I'm at home advertising and recruiting for my team using Gumtree, it was pretty late at night, out of nowhere Jazmine texts asking if I wanted to talk and just chat. Looking back, I knew by accepting this seemingly innocent request that I would be opening a door to temptation, but after working constantly, especially in this work environment that was so demanding, I welcomed the distraction.

We started speaking over the phone for a long time, getting to know each other outside of our work selves. A small flame was ignited that left both of us wanting more, in terms of spending time together. The situation just naturally grew from there and we spent more and more time together, at work and after too. Eventually, we would go on dates, going to restaurants and the cinema. In the beginning, I was my usual non-emotional self with my wall and guard up.

About a year ago, I had dated another girl in the office, on paper the other girl was more suited to me, she was black, her family had a strong background in church too, I even had friends telling me to settle down with her as she was perfect for me. But at the time, I didn't have the mind, desire or maturity to be in a committed relationship. Now, with Jazmine, who was a different race, Indian and different religion, Sikh; my being, emotions and will wanted a relationship with her, even though I was known as the guy who doesn't do relationships.

Time went by and my emotions and feeling had by passed and over-ruled my brain and logic; before I knew it, I had fallen into what I believed to be love at the time. This was something that I had never experienced before, something that I had never aspired for. It just didn't make sense, how did she get here, nobody was supposed to be here. The relationship messed with my head, heart and my spirit. Now that I was in a physical relationship, in my own mind, I was banned from having any relationship with God, how could I? In the past, I would make mistakes and sin, repent and move on, but now I'm living a lifestyle of sin and because I was in love, I wasn't prepared to walk away. In the past when I was younger and less mature, I would and did give up anything that took God's place in my life, but not this time.

Jazmine was the first girlfriend that I introduced to my family, at my mom's house and also at Hill Top. Looking back, for large parts of the relationship, we were living in a "false economy", what I mean by that is, because of the nature of our work, we probably spent an hour after work together and a few hours together on Saturday. We were always in a position where we constantly missed each other, which heightened the excitement and emotions. But of course in a real relationship, normally you spend so much time together to the point where you want a break, you get to know all the annoying habits and so forth, but we never got this, so in a sense it wasn't a real relationship, but this was something I wouldn't understand until later in life. For me, love is a decision, it means knowing someone's bad habits, seeing the absolute worse in a person and still choosing them; we only mainly saw the best versions of ourselves. Another sign was that, although we had a physical relationship, she never knew about my insecurities, like the scar on my arm or ever saw it in 18 months. Nevertheless, all this didn't stop me feeling the way I felt at the time.

There was a constant battle in my mind about being with Jazmine, one was the fact that this was keeping me in a lifestyle that was contrary to what I knew was right and of course, this came with a lot of guilt. Another thing that I battled with was the thought of the end game, as in where was this relationship going? I was still the same guy that when I was a teenager, believed there was no point in entering into a relationship unless the end goal was marriage and I couldn't see how this would work. She came from an Indian background where if an Indian woman married a white man, this was bad, but to be with a black man, was an absolute abomination (in a lot of cases), some families would carry out honour killings. Besides, our whole relationship was hidden from her family. Whenever we were out, we were both on our guard in case we were ever spotted in public together alone. As time went by, this was something that we discussed, she would often say to me that I would be her only family as she knew being with me would effectively mean losing her whole family.

In 2012, after leaving Appco, a couple of short months later, Jazmine would also leave, not long after that, the whole office would shut down under Peter's leadership. So Jazmine and I were both looking for jobs at the same time. During this period, she went on a family holiday to India, when she got back, it wasn't long until she found a job in Birmingham city centre, shortly after I myself got a job at a recruitment company off Colmore Row in Birmingham City Centre, the company was called PT Recruitment. They provided staff for care homes and hostels; my role was to find new care homes to sell to.

Our offices weren't too far from each other, Jazmine would finish work and then jump on the bus for a short journey and meet me. It all felt weird in the beginning, we had been used to finishing work at 11pm every night and catching the last bus home together. Now Jazmine would meet me at my workplace at 5:30 when I finished and we would stay in town and go for a drink or get some food. She could only stay for about an hour as her family were really strict, it's amazing they let her work at Appco when we were working late hours. All the excitement from the beginning of our relationship had seemingly dried up, the honey had left the moon and the honeymoon period was over. Things just seemed different, my guilt levels due to my lifestyle were at an all-time high, I had tried to change our relationship a year prior to a non-physical one, but Jazmine wasn't keen on this. This was something I suggested to try to irradicate all the guilt I had, all why still maintaining the relationship. Now a year on, I was in the same head space and Jazmine was different too. We went through a stage where we would break up and then get back together. One time, I plucked up the courage to actually end things and I tried to solidify my decision by going out with a work colleague and meeting other women, but Jazmine wanted to get back together and I couldn't say no.

Then there was another time that I broke things off, but then it was me that wanted to get back together, but this time Jazmine said no. Her whole character changed and any love that she once had for me had gone. I remember praying months before this, asking God to end the relationship because I didn't have the strength to do it myself because of my feelings and emotions…

"Be careful what you ask for, you might just get it!"

I couldn't understand how and why Jazmine had turned so cold. The revelations that would soon follow would give me all the answers that I needed. It turned out that when she went to India for that 'family holiday', she was actually going to pick out her wedding dress… she was engaged to the boyfriend that I had met a couple of years ago at the Appco awards ceremony. I found out because my friend's girlfriend spent time at Jazmine's house after having nowhere else to go after a domestic abuse incident. The wedding would take place very shortly after we broke up, this was part of the reason why she wouldn't give the relationship another go. I say part of the reason, because at the moment, I realised that Jazmine was a pathological liar. This was very similar when I found out that my dad cheated on my mom, only this time I was the one who had been cheated on.

One day after work at PT Recruitment, everyone goes out for a drink, it's good weather and everyone is having a good time, I'm slightly inebriated and I get a call from my friend, the same friend who's girlfriend stayed at Jazmine's house, he starts telling me more information about the whole situation, this was when I found out more details about the wedding, the trip to India, how the family are putting up decorations for the wedding. I put the phone down and tell God, "It takes me 40 mins to get home, you have 40 minutes to convince not to go onto to social media and expose Jazmine to her family and husband," in my head, if they knew she had been in a physical relationship with a black man for 18 months, that would be enough to stop the wedding and ruin her life. I get on the metro and get on the connecting bus, partially full of alcohol, rage and anger. I could have killed this girl and comfortably spent 26 years in prison, it would be a great way to really connect to God, plus there's no women, so that's 90% of my temptation eliminated. I would all but be guaranteed a place in heaven.

"If you haven't contemplated murder, you ain't been in love."
– Chris Rock

I get home at Hill Top, but I decide not to do anything. I'm angry with myself for being so stupid, I'm angry with God for seeing all this and not warning me; it's funny how we walk away from God, make our own decisions and then blame Him for the consequences in our lives. Then last but not least, I'm angry with Jazmine. Till this day I have never had the chance to speak to her to ask her any questions and understand any of this, to get some form of closure. It's like she got off scot-free. She got married almost straight after we broke up and had a honeymoon in Cancun, I couldn't believe the injustice! I'm meant to be the Christian and have favour with God, but it sure didn't feel that way. She was living her new life and I was heartbroken and devasted. My friend had once said, "There's no greater pain than the pain of heartbreak," I didn't understand at the time, but boy did I understand at this point in my life. I had this pain that I had never felt. It felt like I couldn't breathe, I was being suffocated with grief, pain, loneliness and negativity. I felt very unstable, like I could just breakdown at any moment.

I started losing hair and had a bald patch on the top of my head, at first I just thought it was genetic as my dad was bald and so were both of my grandads, but it was stress as the hair would later grow back. One time during this heart break period, I was on the metro and I literally thought I was having a heart attack, it was like something was squeezing my heart from the inside and I couldn't sit still. I would have many ECGs, but that would be the start of a series of heart palpitations. I would be somewhere, and they would start and I would get short of breath and I would have panic attacks. I was a broken man who didn't know he was broken or how to put myself back together. My drinking drastically ramped up, it was like drinking and being drunk numbed the pain. I drank every day after work and sometimes never made it home. I drank heavily at home and drank heavily on family holidays, I was in emotional pain and depressed, but didn't know it. Back then mental health wasn't as big as it is today. I just tried to continue. Again, there was no one to show me how to deal with heart break, so I had to figure it out by myself.

This pain would last for about 3–4 months, until I went onto a family holiday to Florida, back then there were about 22 of us from my mom's side that would go. After months and months of pain, one day on the holiday, I woke up early, I went outside by the pool by myself and God began to speak to me and I just wrote down everything word for word. As He was speaking to me, it was like he was doing surgery on me and removing the pain, heart break anger and bitterness. Up until this point, I still had no answers to all my questions and no closure, but in that moment, God gave me closure with his peace that passes all understanding. He taught me that you can get closure and close up wounds without speaking to the person who caused the offence. I was emotionally healed! I remember friends asking me how I got over the situation so easily and quickly and I explained that it was through God and shared the words he gave me. From this point, I would come back fully to church and my relationship with God just grew and grew.

Chapter Reflections

- *Have you ever opened the door to things, that at the face of it looked innocent, but deep down you knew it would take you down a wrong path? What did you learn from the experience?*
- *Have you ever fallen in love with someone that you knew you couldn't and shouldn't be with? If so, what was the outcome and what did you learn?*
- *Have you been in a situation where someone has caused you hurt/offence and it felt like they just got away with it with zero consequences? How did you handle the injustice?*

Chapter 13
The New Normal

After the break-up and heart break from my relationship with Jazmine, although I felt healed emotionally, it didn't stop me feeling lonely and lost. When you have had a routine in your life for a period of time, you are now conditioned and anything outside of your normal routine feels alien. After work, I would meet Jazmine and go for food or for a drink, now work was over and I would go straight home for a period, I felt lost. Weekends were awful as I just didn't know what to do with myself. I couldn't imagine being with another person, I couldn't imagine being happy single when I had just come out of my longest and only real relationship.

Not only was I dealing with a new normal in terms of Jazmine, I was dealing with a new normal with my dad. The year before, I believe it was 2011, I had hit a major bump in the road with my relationship with my dad. Because I was always working at Appco all the hours in the world, I didn't really notice my parent's relationship, especially as I was now living at Hill Top.

One day I'm at Hill Top and my parents ask to speak to me privately upstairs in my grandparents' room. My mom is sitting on one corner of the bed and my dad is at the opposite side kind of sitting and resting on the dressing table. I'm wondering what's happening. My dad starts talking, he says that he and my mom are splitting up… again. The last time we had a conversation like this outside of McDonalds, I was an innocent church boy with the fruit of the Spirit, this time I was in a very different head space. I ask the question, "So what happened? You don't just wake up one day and say we should split, something must have happened for you both to come to this decision…" My dad responds and says that they both gave it a try but it's just not working. I look into the other corner of the room where my mom is sitting silent. I look back at my dad, seven years ago when we spoke outside McDonalds, there was no eye contact from either of us, this time as I am speaking, my eyes are piercing and speaking louder than the words coming out of my mouth. I look my dad in the eye and say, "You cheated again?" It was a mixture of a question and a statement. My dad responds and confirms. I have this rage and fire inside me, "So if I never asked, you would have let me and other people believe that it's mutual?" Everyone in the room knew that my mom would never bad mouth my dad or expose him, just like the last time it happened.

I was absolutely fuming without God to help filter my response. "So let me get this right, you cheat on Mom, mess her about and then run off; then you come back, mess with her again and now you're off again?" At that time, I was in my first ever proper relationship, so I couldn't imagine how a man could do that to a girlfriend, let alone a wife. As you can imagine, this affected my relationship with my dad. It was the fact that he could just go back to work in London and live a different life, while the rest of us are left to pick up the pieces.

My dad was now in relationship with someone else, time went by, but I believe it was all in the same year as I was still with Jazmine at the time. I don't remember how we got back on speaking terms, but somehow we were. My dad had got tickets for this Olympic event taking place in Perry Barr. It was on a Saturday, I remember because I was sacrificing spending time with Jazmine to meet my dad, this was in Appco days where I rarely had spare time. If I remember correctly, my dad and I were working on building back our relationship. The day starts off good, we watched some of the running sports, I think it was a 100M sprint followed by other sports. My dad says we should go get some food, so we leave the event to go across the street to the shop. After we eat, we start walking back, my dad starts speaking about his new girlfriend. The conversation comes up about if I would be interested in meeting her, I abruptly decline. I mentioned before that my dad had a habit of forcing his will on others; I was told that he met up with his cousin Colin and without asking him, arranged for his new girlfriend to show up. Colin wasn't happy with this and when his wife Sadie found out, she wasn't either. This was a pattern that I would see now and again in the future, where my dad was just do whatever he wants, despite how it made other people feel. So when he asks if I want to meet his girlfriend, that's why I abruptly answered to shut it down and indicate for him to never do to me what he did to Colin.

As we are walking back into the event, my dad continues to talk, he says how his girlfriend was meant to be here at the event with him, but couldn't get a sitter for her cat, so that's why he had the spare ticket for me to come. I start filling up with rage again. Before speaking, I start to process what I've just heard before I speak. In my mind I'm saying, "So you mean to tell me, the only reason why you wanted to spend time with me, was because your girlfriend, who, alongside yourself mashed up the family, couldn't make it? So I'm just a last resort, and after thought... okay then..." At this point, I had done enough processing and was ready to speak. Everything that I was thinking, I tell him, I stop walking back inside event and turn around and walk off to the bus stop, I was done. It just felt like my dad didn't care about anyone but himself, surely he couldn't be this blind or naïve to how his words and actions would affect others around him, especially his family, the ones he should be guarding and protecting.

Time goes by and we arrange to speak at Hilltop, I had questions that I wanted answering. I literally wrote down all my questions on my phone so I wouldn't forget anything. The night before Mommy Fletcher and I were speaking. I spoke to her about the whole situation and asked her how she felt and what her thoughts were. She tells me about her life experiences, her relationship with her father and the fact that she too had half siblings – I had no idea! This is why it's good for families to talk and I mean talk properly. Mommy Fletcher was a laid-back person anyway and easily forgave, but I wasn't ready to do that. I asked her if my dad ever apologised to her for what he did to her daughter, she responds and says no. "So how can you be okay when he comes here, then has the audacity to bring my half-sister without first apologising and most importantly asking you if it's okay for her to come?" She shrugs her shoulders as though it's a minor thing.

She said, "Sometimes people don't verbally say they are sorry, but you can see it and sense it in their behaviour and how they speak." She was too understanding for my liking, I wanted someone that would join me in my anger and help fan the fire.

The next day, my dad arrives at Hill Top. We go upstairs to talk, I didn't know what to expect or how this would go. The conversation starts okay at first, I don't know if my emotions got the best of me or if my dad's politician 'round the houses', long-winded, 'I'm going to talk in riddles and make you forget the question' answers were winding me up. It's like he wouldn't answer questions directly. It got quite heated to the point where we both just walked off. Some time went by before we would speak again, it was like there was a series of events taken place in a short time.

At Christmas that year, or the year either side of that year, my dad was meant to come to Hill Top for Christmas day, but this year would be different. My dad said he wouldn't make it to the Midlands Christmas Day because his girlfriend wanted him to spend the day with her. When I heard this, it felt like another blow, for me it felt like rejection after rejection, after rejection. It was like he was stabbing his family, then constantly twisting the knife. For me, if you're going to make decisions like this and pick a woman over your wife and children, you HAVE to make that relationship work, so at least psychologically it was 'worth it' in some way. But to do that and then for the relationship to end quite quickly, it's like you're hurting us for nothing. Now from that point moving on, every Christmas that you spend with your family, I am forever thinking that you're doing this because we are the only option left, just like when we went to the Olympic event in Perry Barr.

What confused me and made me angry was, from my perspective, my dad was using my mom, that's from that period and for the next 10 years. Eventually, my dad would go from working away in London, then internationally to Ireland, Scandinavia and then eventually USA, until he would live there in the future. So when he would fly into the country, my mom would pick him up from the airport or train station. When he was in the UK, he would always have and use her car. He would go back to his old marriage home, where my mom would sort out food for him. It was like they were married again for the two weeks or however long he was here. This would be an ongoing thing, where the family would be back to 'normal', then he would leave again. This was mentally draining, unhealthy and psychologically damaging. It seemed like whenever my dad needed emotional support, it wouldn't come from his girlfriends, if it did, it wasn't enough as he would always go to my mom. This is something that I watched for years, everyone in the immediate family seemed to be fine with how things were and at that point I felt like I was the only one that had negative feelings.

My dad would speak to my mom more than he spoke to me, Christian and Calesha. I didn't understand this. Because of this, the things that he knew about us, was came from conversations with my mom as opposed to our own relationship, this was something that I hated. I would often tell my mom to stop telling my dad about me and that if he wants to know anything, he should call me.

I understood that he chose to walk away from his marriage and divorce, but you can't divorce your children. I couldn't understand how a parent wouldn't want to be around their children and would choose themselves over their own children. When we speak about a parent's protection for their children, I think of a parent taking a bullet for their child or throwing themselves in harm's way so their child can escape, but at this stage in my life it just felt rejection and abandonment. This was a feeling that lasted for years… The feelings towards my dad were the same as before, whenever he wasn't there I had feelings of anger, resentment and injustice, but when he would come into the country I had feelings of mercy and compassion, I think because I thought that he too must be suffering emotionally and feeling guilty. It was confusing and there wasn't a manual of how to deal with it all.

It was around this time, that another miracle happened in my family on my mom's side. In 2011, I was deep in my own world and not attending the family prayer meeting, but the prayers never stopped. This was a miracle that I only heard about as I was totally wrapped up with work at Appco. My uncle Mark's wife Mia got pregnant, but during the pregnancy there were some serious complications. On a Sunday Morning getting ready for church, Mia notice that she had started bleeding. At this point, she had already had her 12-week scan. They both immediately went to A&E, where they were told that they may have lost the baby, at this time they had not done a scan. Mia was advised that she needed to stay overnight and the following morning they would do a D&E (dilation and evacuation). Paperwork was signed for the procedure to take place the next day!

This would have and should have been the end of the story, but there's something about a praying woman and a praying man, who come together and touch and agree in prayer.

"It's not over until God says it's over, He has the final say!"

Mike and Mia contact people on both sides of the family who have faith and know how to pray. They explain the situation, but the people that are listening aren't phased by the situation nor by the doctor's words. So prayer and fasting takes place immediately.

Even now, as I look back, if I take off my 'Christian' hat, this is absolutely crazy and must be part of the grieving process. If a medical doctor tells you that someone is dead, that is fact! So to believe against all the facts is crazy and foolishness.

"This foolish plan of God is wiser than the wisest of human plans, and God's weakness is stronger than the greatest of human strength." 1 Corinthians 1:25 (NLT)

That same night whilst saying the Lord's Prayer Mia felt a flutter in her stomach. With all the faith that she has in her body and soul she says, "Thank you God." This is faith!

The next morning, a senior doctor who Mia had never seen before came to see her and examined her. She then said, "Mrs Fletcher, I just want to take you down to do one more check." Unaware, she had taken her to the exact same scan room where Mike and Mia had previously been told that they had lost their little baby boy Hayden in 2004. In all honestly, to have to relive that same moment and be in the exact situation and in the exact same room, should have stolen, killed and destroyed any faith that they had… but God! In that moment, Mia did not show any emotion but a peace fell upon her.

"Then you will experience God's peace, which exceeds anything we can understand. His peace will guard your hearts and minds as you live in Christ Jesus." Philippians 4:7 (NLT)

Mia was prepared for the scan and then she heard the doctor say, "Mrs Fletcher, there's your baby jumping around". They both began praising God. The prayers amongst the families during that time was covering the situation. Nicholas Samuel Fletcher was born at 12.47pm on Wednesday 9th May 2012 weighing 8lbs 12oz.

Time and time again in my life, I have witnessed God's power in my life and my family's. I love when God does something like this, because no one else can take the credit and there's no shadow of a doubt that there was divine intervention.

Following on from my breakup with Jazmine and the family holiday that year, as previously mentioned, I started a job at PT recruitment. This was the start of my new normal, before breaking up with Jazmine and was a whole adventure in and of itself…

Chapter Reflections

- *Have you ever had a breakup? If so, how did you adjust to your new life and routine?*
- *Do you have unresolved issues with any of your parents (particularly your father), if so, what have you done to try and deal with the problem?*

Chapter 14
Character Development

When I first started working at PT Recruitment, everything was new and exciting. I was earning a lot more money than I was at Appco and it was a guaranteed salary which was alien to me. Even getting paid once a month, instead of weekly was weird at first. I was still living at Hill Top and my monthly expenses were next to nothing, so after I paid my bills, I had a lot of money left over and I didn't know what to do with it. At this stage of my life, I was very much financially immature and wasn't thinking about savings or my future, I just wanted to enjoy life and the 'here and now'.

One of the first things I did was buy my mom an iPad, she had been talking about how she wanted one, but it was quite expensive, so I surprised her on her birthday and she loved it. I wrapped it up and told her it was perfume and when she opened it, I can still see the look of surprise and excitement on her face now.

At PT Recruitment, there were two offices in one, our office dealt with social care and the other office dealt with another sector. On my team, there were a lot of black people, in fact more black people that white, which I liked as it made me feel more comfortable. All the staff were women and were in their late 30s or higher. Some of the key people to me were Megan, Heather and Ron, to this day, 10 years later we are all still in touch and meet up once or twice a year.

At first Megan and I got off on the wrong foot, I made joke about not wanting to go to London carnival as I didn't want to get killed, which Megan didn't like because I was making black people look bad to the white staff members. We spoke about it and I got what she meant, but she never got my sense of humour and thought I was being serious, but as time went by she got to know when I was serious and when I was joking.

Heather, back then, was the first one in the office, she would get there at 7:30ish even though work started at 9am. She was a real team player and always gave 100%, she was always happy and smiling, I don't recall seeing her angry or upset.

Ron joined as an apprentice, he was 17 years old at the time, he was and still is like a little brother to me and everyone else. He was highly intelligent, and we had the same sense of humour. Just like me, as time went on, he didn't care about his job at PT Recruitment. I remember one time, we were out in the city centre for lunch, we were walking and talking and then he just disappeared. I carried on back to the office, as lunch time was almost over and didn't want to be late. Ron's manager was asking everyone if they had seen him, as we were now almost three hours past lunch time. Then he called Ron's parents as he was concerned about his safety. Not long after that, Ron casually walked into the office from the cinema, he had watched a film, he just didn't care and eventually my mindset towards PT Recruitment would reach there.

The manager at PT Recruitment was a guy called Adam, I only met him on my first day starting, he never interviewed me, it was his manager, Jake. Jake and I got on well together, he liked the fact that I had worked in an environment for three years with no basic salary, totally dependent on commission, plus my other leadership skills. In my interview, he told me that I could easily do his job.

From my first day meeting Adam, we never really clicked like I did with other people. At first, I thought it was because of what I could bring to the table, especially after my issues with my last manager Patrick in Appco. If this was to be the case, then I would be ready. I had promised myself after everything I went through with Peter, the bullying, intimidation, the anxiety and sleepless nights, that NO ONE would ever have that power over me again or make me feel that way again.

As we got into 2013, I found out at an after work even that Amy, another salesperson, hired around the same time as me was on more money than me, even though we were doing the same job and I was out performing her. I remember meeting Amy for the first time in 2012, Adam brought us into another room to do some training with us. When he left the room to get some handouts, Amy and I started speaking, asking each other about our work history and so forth, at that time I mentioned that I had a girlfriend, then Amy said, "Phew, that's good to know." She was implying that because I had a girlfriend that there would be no chance of my approaching her for any type of office romance. When I heard that, it stuck with me, it made me feel that I was perceived as some type of predator, and I was someone that should be feared and watched. It was around this time that I would catch the bus and then the metro to work. Every morning, I would see the same people at the bus stop, some were women. As we would wait for the bus, I would very consciously stand well away from the women and make sure I was in their eye line, so they could see me and any movements that I would make. I felt I needed to do this to make them feel safe in my presence so they too could say, "Phew."

> *"Things from our past can subconsciously control our future, for better or worse."*

Now because I found out that Amy was on more money than me, that instantly drained all my motivation for the job, on top of that it was near enough impossible to make any commission. There was no one in the company that did my role that made commission, so mentally I was done. I think it was pretty evident to most people that I stopped caring and this would start the next series of events. As a company, they would go through a lot of salespeople and when they no longer wanted them, they would either fire of manage them out of the business. Most salespeople at this stage would either not care and leave, or not have the knowledge of how to deal with a situation like this.

So one day, I get a letter from the company which basically says they will manage me out of the business based on performance. They set a date for a meeting with me and three other managers, Adam, Jake who hired me and Molly, a newly promoted manager. To this day, I don't understand why they needed a 3 vs 1 meeting, must have been to try and intimidate me, but they didn't know what I had experienced at Appco and my no-nonsense policy about such things. I didn't mind leaving, as I didn't care about the job, for me, it was all about the principal, and I would leave when I and I alone decided.

I told my family about the situation, this became a big focus on the Monday night prayer meetings, every week I would update the family as we prayed and fasted. My aunty Sally told me about joining a union. Normally, you have to already be with a union before you call on them for assistance, you couldn't just sign up and them for an existing case, but Sally had friend at the union. The meeting at PT Recruitment was set for Monday morning, I had spoken with Sally's contact, Gavin on the Friday. I explained briefly what the situation was and he informed me that from a legal perspective, we have the right to decline the meeting and request another date, so that we have time to prepare everything.

On Monday morning, I go to work, work starts at 9am and the meeting was scheduled for around 9:30am, it was early morning. At around 9:15am, the managers get up laughing and talking with each other, as they go to the meeting room to most likely discuss my demise. At this point, head office hadn't updated them on my request through my union that the meeting would not be taking place. Around 10 minutes later, the three managers walk back into the office, this time there's no laughter or banter and they glance over to me as they take their seats.

Once I had the chance to meet with Gavin, I explained the situation of how they had given me a target that was five times more than other sales people in and out of our office and I had the evidence. I went on to explain that they had put me on a performance plan to 'help me', but the plan expected me to achieve more than I was before the plan was introduced. The whole idea is to give smaller targets, if you owe a bank £5,000 and the monthly payment is £250, then they say that they are willing to support you and ask for £300 per month, then clearly that's not helping, that's making things worse. I explained this in the first official meeting between PT Recruitment and my union, with evidence, showing their true intent to manage me out of the business.

I raised more grievances, based on solid facts, backed up by evidence. This meant that I had to call people out and that they would in turn not only hate me, but make it their mission to get back at me. The whole process would go on to last around eight months.

When the first meeting took place, it was Gavin and I on one side and then Jake, the one who hired me and PT Recruitment's HR manager. It was a very intense meeting, this was something new for me and a definite character development opportunity. I remember in the meeting speaking about one of my grievances which related to Jake and having to look him in the eye. Had I not gone through what I went through with Patrick at Appco, I don't think I would have been mentally strong enough to says the things that I said.

The meeting as a whole went okay, I got to say everything that I wanted, but I still felt dissatisfied. In the meeting, I was totally reliant on me and all the facts that I had worked so hard on producing. I learned my lesson. The next meeting, I wouldn't go in with notes, I was determined to rely on God and his guidance. I went on a few days fasting and my family joined me. I'll never forget the day of that second meeting, I got off the metro at Snow Hill and did my usual five minute walk, but this time, it felt like two angels were on either side of me accompanying me. I get to work and go to the toilet and pray some more.

Gavin wasn't able to attend this meeting, so instead he sent Grant, who acted in a capacity for the union itself. When Grant walks in and I meet him for the first time, he is very unassuming. I expected him to talk through the plan for the meeting and clarify some points with me, but instead he spoke about his neighbour's garden, it was like he wasn't prepared and didn't care about the meeting. It was so bad, that at one point, I though PT Recruitment had hired an actor to pretend to be my union rep. But as we went into the meeting, all my doubts would be quickly withdrawn, Grant knew employment law like a pastor knows their Bible and he could not only quote the law, but also the section and sub-section. PT Recruitment's HR interrupted Grant as he was speaking, she did the same thing in the last meeting, but this time Grant spoke in a calm soft voice and quoted the law which explains that in a meeting type, such as ours, you can't interrupt people and if you do more than 'X' times, we can end the end the meeting and report back. He completely subdued everyone and everyone in the room was in awe of not only his knowledge, but his temperament and delivery.

By the end of the meeting, we were in full control, the whole situation had turned on its head, from them looking to fire me, to me raising grievances and discussing a pay-out for my distress.

In the background of all this happening, I was looking for a new role and been offered a new job for more money. As soon as I accepted the new job, handed in my notice and left with my head held high, with a nice hefty pay out from PT Recruitment.

"... If God is for us, who can be against us." Romans 8:31 (NIV)

When I left, someone mentioned my name and Jake said, "Don't mention that name again in this office," this was the first time they had come across someone like me, an educated black man, who knew how to handle himself and knows God. I remember during that time, people at work asking me how I was dealing with all this as, they would have had a breakdown. At the time I felt pretty much okay during the period, but looking back now, I realise how intense the situation was. It was like God was protecting my mind and heart.

Towards the end of me leaving PT Recruitment, they hired a woman, who we'll call Princess, that was her nick name. During this stage, I was highly paranoid of all the managers. One of the guys in the office had heard the managers speaking about me and warned me. When we were going through the whole tribunal saga, I would have meetings with Adam where he would have another manager there to witness everything. Once I found out that he was talking about me to other managers, I raised this, and stated that I would be choosing the people who would sit in on my meetings moving forward.

On another occasion, I started get palpitations, these started following my breakup with Jazmine, so I left work to go to the doctors, which I told Adam about. After leaving the doctors, Adam called me to ask where I was, to my surprise. He said he had no idea where I was and that he wasn't told. So these are some of the games they were playing.

So when Princess started, she was almost like a male version of me in terms of personality and we got on really well, it seemed too good to be true that we had so much in common and just got on. I literally believed that PT Recruitment hired her just to get close to me and find out things about me and my plans with my union and I was serious.

When Princess started, I was in church and focused, especially because I had this whole tribunal situation happening, amongst the fact that I had been totally reliant on God after my breakup with Jasmine. There was a mutual attraction between Princess and I, but I was NOT entering into another relationship with anyone else, especially after everything I had been through.

One day after work, Princess and I go for a drink at a Wetherspoons in the city centre. I remember this like it was yesterday, I specifically told her, that I categorically do not want a relationship, but I'm happy to be friends, almost as a disclaimer to protect myself from any future liability. This was something that would be addressed by my manager at my new job, Celsian Education.

From here, I spent a lot of time speaking with Princess in the office and on the phone after work. One day, I meet Princess at Slug & Lettuce in Harborne, close to where she lives. We have a good time and end up kissing, but still in my mind, I have set the boundaries and said, "No relationship." Princess had her own flat and lived by herself, it wasn't long before I was practically in a carbon copy situation, just like I was with Naomi five years prior.

Being around Princess, although in my mind, we were just friends, was just too much temptation. Eventually, I would eventually back slide and leave church again. Just like with Naomi, I would stay over at Princess's flat, she would make dinner, go to the market and buy things that I liked and then cook for me. She wanted an official title of being a couple, whereas I didn't.

Looking back, I can see that I slipped back into a place where my mental health was very low, I knew this because I tried to start smoking weed again, something that I hadn't done for almost 10 years. On top of that, I had the guilt again of being intimate but being a Christian. Eventually, I had to end things, as the relationship wasn't good for me or fair to Princess. I told her that I want to go back to church and could only be with a church girl, which she could never understand. I felt incredibly bad, as I felt like I had messed with her head and her heart.

When I joined Celsian Education in early 2014, my manager Simone, spoke to me about Princess. At Celsian, people openly spoke about their relationships and we had some good discussions. I remember telling Simone, who at the time was dating and wanted to be married, that I had told Princess that I only want to be friends, so it's not my fault if she gets feelings. Simone explained that I was saying one thing, but my actions and my relationship with Princess were saying something else, so naturally Princess would get emotionally invested and that I have to take responsibility for that. This was a lesson for me and further character development. From that point on, I was very careful how I interacted with women, as I didn't want the same thing happening again, I would be more intentional in the future.

After breaking up Princess, I felt better in myself, now I could just focus on me and church. When I first join Celsian Education, everything is going well, and I am performing far past everyone's expectations. On my first 'Sale', we provided supply teachers and teaching assistants on long term and short-term bookings; on my first 'sale'/booking, I secured two teachers in one go, it was so good, the regional manager, Linda, Simone's boss came in the office and gave me a big kiss on the cheek. Other people in the office commented that they had never seen anyone perform so well in such a short period time, I remember Simone saying that they should increase my target. Everything was going well at this time.

During this period, or later that year, there was a big issue at my church. The year before, 2013, before Princess came on the scene, I was focused and doing well – however you determine what that looks like. All my life in church, I felt like I was hidden or invisible in Bethel, my church organisation. I remember being a teenager and always seeing other people my age pushed forward or being used on a national scale, but I wasn't even heard of. This frustrated me because firstly, the people pushed forward, in most cases didn't offer much when they were given the chance or were only there based on who their parents were or the church they attended, so it was based on church status, rather than anointing or calling.

Another reason why it annoyed me, was because, ever since I heard the prophecy over my life, I was always looking for how it would transpire and thought it had to come through the church pulpit. In 2013, I had my first semi reveal to the Bethel organisation. There was a Central District Young People's meeting, and it would take place at my church and I was asked to speak. There was a separate meeting the week before for all the different Young People's leaders, to decide a theme and who would be speaking. The theme was 'Called to Duty', as soon as I heard the title, God downloaded everything that I would say, when I was my turn to speak. That was always the pattern, seek God, let Him speak, then copy and paste it.

On the night of the meeting, I had fasted all day, I remember being at home and practising and going through my topic and feeling the anointing and power. When I spoke that night, God worked through me and His word was powerful, after I spoke, the service shifted and someone prophesised. When it came time for the main preacher to speak, he said, "Who was that young man that spoke?" This was the first time that I had a proper opportunity to speak somewhat properly at a Bethel meeting. That summer, because people had heard me speak, I was asked to speak at our yearly convention at Kelvin Way, I don't know if it was to be the main speaker or to speak in a different capacity. In my mind, this would be part of the journey to fulfilling the prophecy, either way, it was something that wouldn't take place.

Sometime before the national convention meeting, there was a national women's meeting at Kelvin Way, my aunty Polly and my mom, were serving on the team at a national and local level respectively, so they were required to attend. However, there was a message from our Pastor that no one should go to Kelvin Way but should come to our home church and for all those they don't, "for every action, there's opposite and equal reaction" – that was the statement made. Now to me, I didn't care either way. I was still living at Hill Top, but every so often I would go home to my mom's and stay over. That weekend, I stayed at my mom's, because I didn't drive at that point, I would go wherever my mom went, so out of respect and courtesy, I messaged my Pastor to let him know that I would be attending the national women's meeting. At the time, I believe I was newly appointed at the Young People's president of our church.

I got a text back almost immediately, explaining that I was no longer the Young People's president based on me going to Kelvin Way. I didn't know what to think or what to say, so I did nothing.

I felt out of place at church, because apart from the text, there was no instruction of what this meant, was I allowed to be used in church? How long would this punishment last for? Was I allowed to join in when it was testimony time? I had no clue and wasn't approached about what would happen next.

Around this time, Liam reached out to me, he told me he had left his church in Oldbury for another one in Aston called New Jerusalem. I told him about my current situation, and he invited me to New J. On the Sunday, he picked me up and we went together, when I got to the church, it was worship time and the worship team were awesome, I had never heard anything like it live. I instantly fell in love with the church. They were so organised from the moment you walked in, being greeted by the ushers. It was very professional. Part way through the service, the Bishop of the church walked in with his armour bearer, he was dressed in a nice suit and when he spoke, it was very relatable and relevant. The congregation were nice too, people made me feel welcome.

After service, Liam and I went downstairs in the kitchen for refreshments, not long after the Bishop came down, his name was Bishop Melvin Brooks. He introduced himself to me and asked how I was doing in life and where I was from. In that one conversation, he knew more about than most people at my current church, that's not to say I wasn't looked after at my current church, but to emphasise how much of a people person Bishop Brooks is and if you have ever met him, you would know this to be true.

I left that day, almost already deciding to leave my church and move to New J, I would continue to visit New J a few more times. One of the things that helped make my decision was seeing Elder Keith there, I remember as boy listening to him preach at Gibson Road and 'mashing up' the place. Plus, when he moved to Canada, he stayed with Mommy Fletcher' sister, aunty Sonia, so he was well known by the family. So in my mind, if it's good enough for Elder Keith, it's good enough for me.

I remember praying to God about moving and him telling me I had bitterness in my heart towards my current pastor based on recent events. I was told I couldn't leave in my current state and that I need to pray and fast for three days to deal with it.

On the day that I had decided to do my first day of fasting, I spoke to my pastor at church and explained that I would be leaving and moving on. He asked me for one thing; to fast for three days before making my decision, this was perfect as I was already doing this at the time and on my second out of the three days, so I agreed. Once I finished my fasting, I wrote a letter and sent it to my old pastor and officially started attending New J, a few weeks later, I took the right hand of fellowship, which is something you do when you become an official member. On that day, I invited all my family, a lot of them enjoyed the service and liked New J and several of them also joined me.

My sister and brother started coming, eventually my sister decided to get baptised and became heavily involved with the youth team and worship team. My brother started coming and eventually got involved with the media team and made good friends with other like-minded boys. Mike and Mia came, Mia got involved with the new converts class and Mike got involved with the other men who help with security and hospitality. My Uncle Gerald started attending, he would stay for a few years before moving on, in his few years at New J, my cousin Dean, his and my aunty Polly's son got baptised too.

"And we know that God causes everything to work together for the good…"
Romans 8:28 (NLT)

Through all the mess during this period of me leaving and finding a new church, a lot of good came from it and I'm glad it happened this way.

Chapter Reflections

- What things have you experienced in the past, that to this day affect the way that you act?
- Have you ever parted way with a person, job or organisation? If so, did you leave on good terms? Reflect…

Chapter 15
Character Development Part Two

During this stage of my life, God was really working on my character and refining me more and more. He was teaching me that my character was paramount and that my gifts, talents and abilities should never outweigh my character. I had seen people who were heavily gifted and talented mess up opportunities and/or their life due to a lack of character.

I was still at Celsian Education and was performing well, but my character still needed work and I would get an attitude adjustment. People in my family would always tell me that I was a very direct, no-nonsense person with a sometimes-aggressive demeanour, in terms of my communication, but I never really paid them any mind. But my manager Simone would tell me everything that my family had been speaking about.

One day, Simone called a meeting with me and Linda, her manager. She wanted to speak to me about my conduct in the office and boy was she ready, as she pulled out a list and went through each point, her emotions got the better of her and I could see that these things had really been bothering her and she didn't know how to deal with the situation. This was a very humbling experience, having to sit there and listen to someone tell you multiple bad traits that you have, but I had to humble myself and take it all on the chin. To be fair, how Linda ran the meeting was very skilful and how she put her points across, I couldn't argue or try to talk my way out. Although I was the one being dealt with, I was also learning how to communicate and deal with issues with other people. After the meeting, I would intentionally choose the tone that I would use when calling Simone's name, this was one of the things she never liked, she said the way I called her name in the office was very aggressive and forceful.

After the meeting, things seemed to get better. One day, one of my accounts calls for business, everyone had their own accounts. I was on the phone, so

Simone took the call for me and took down the request but kept it for herself. I didn't know how to respond, as I was previously told that I was too aggressive, so didn't know how to communicate the fact that you're stealing my business in a way that was suitable to her. On top of that, I had been there a while and still not earned any commission, so I was ready to leave as I wanted more money and more from a job.

I started looking for a new role, I wanted to leave recruitment but didn't know what else to do. Shortly after, I get a message from a guy who works for another recruitment company based in Wolverhampton town centre. We arrange an interview one day after work and I meet him at his office. His name was Matt, he was a really nice guy who had big plans for his office. I hadn't seen ambition and drive like that since Appco, which I loved. Additionally, this role would increase my salary by £7K a year, so it was a no brainer for me. So after a year at Celsian Education, I left and joined PTL Education Recruitment in March of 2015.

It was here that I would get some real character development. From the moment I started, it was an uphill battle, they already had other sales people there that had been there for years and obviously had all the best clients, so me and another new starter were given whatever else was left over – the scraps. I honestly gave my all in that role but struggled, I would come in an hour earlier just to make more phone calls and do everything that I could to improve my performance, but nothing changed. I prayed and begged God for favour and to help me daily, but nothing changed. It was here that I learned a crucial life lesson.

"If you do everything that you can and you pray and fast, if it doesn't work out, it's not meant for you."

At the time, I never had this revelation, so I thought I did something wrong and God was angry with me and then I started doubting my own ability as a sales person. After seven months, my manager calls me into a room and tells me it's not working out and that he has to let me go. We had a really good personal relationship, he was religious too, we would have discussions about God and ask each other questions. So when he was letting me go he had tears in his eyes and tried to hold them back. He saw that I was trying and demonstrating all the right behaviours, but it just wasn't working. Then he asks if I wanted to go straight home, wait till the end of the day and leave like nothing has happened to avoid saying bye to everyone, or just be open and say bye to people. I chose the latter; I liked the people in the office, so it wouldn't sit right with me just leaving.

I was really confused at the time and felt lost as a whole. I know now that this was God's way of telling me that the recruitment industry was not for me, but that was all I knew and didn't know where to turn. It wasn't long before I found a new role, in fact I was in a position after a few interviews where I had two job offers. Both were recruitment roles in the education sector, the same as Celsian and PTL Education. One was based in Birmingham city and the other was a home-based role, where I would travel to Nottingham once or twice a week. In the end, I went for the home-based role, the company was called TP Education. They set me up with a laptop and all the home equipment that I would need.

When I first start, I hit the ground running and place two overseas teachers, in this role, they looked at teachers on an international level, so I was interviewing people in Australia, Europe, North and South America, as well as Jamaica and the UK. Everything was going well in terms of my performance, and I loved working from home and spending time in Nottingham.

Meanwhile, at my new church, New J, I was still in the honeymoon stage where everything was brand new. The Pastor, Pastor Yvette, who was Bishop Brook's wife announced in church that if anyone is interested in getting involved in ministry or wants help identifying what their ministry is, they could book a meeting with her. I book a meeting and it's the first time that we get to speak properly, she asked about my experiences and also gave me this questionnaire to fill out, it was multiple choice and then at the end you calculate all you answers and it shows you your top three areas of ministry, which I found fascinating, it confirmed what I was already thinking. As I was a 30-year-old single man, Pastor Yvette asked if I was ready or looking to get married, I told her I wasn't at the time, I was just trying to adjust to the church and find my feet with my new job. She told me to let her know when I was ready and that I should make a plan or a list of the things that I am looking for in a wife. I told her that I had already made a plan for my entire life, including a wife, as I met a man around six years ago who told me to do so.

I went home to go over the qualities that I was looking for in a woman. I find the book that I had from six years ago at the retreat that I attended. As I read through the notes and look at my life's plan that I made, I realise that the man who gave me the advice was Bishop Brooks! I totally forgot, as I met him for the first time at the retreat and forgot who he was and what he looked like.

I organised another meeting with Pastor Yvette to further discuss ministry. As we were in the office, Elder Keith walked in, he didn't know that we were having a meeting. Since joining New J, I had been attending Elder Keith's Thursday night Bible class which I loved, I was there almost every week, pestering Elder Keith with question upon question, upon question. We both had a background in Bethel and knew the Bible pretty well. So as he walks and sees me, he jokingly says, "Rabbi," which is a person who knows the word of God.

Pastor Yvette looks at us both as if to say, "Why are you calling him Rabbi?" Then Elder Keith explains. Pastor Yvette responds and says there is a men's night next Sunday, where different men will be giving a short word and asked if I would like to speak, I agreed.

"A man's gift makes room for him and brings him before the great." Proverbs 18:16 (ESV)

Just like that, I had an opportunity to speak. When I first moved to New J, my only reservation was, how will I be able to use my gift and grow. In my old church, I had plenty of opportunity to speak and grow and develop, but at New J, only the leaders would preach, or at least that was my own personal observation, but now this became a moot point.

On the men's Sunday, I was given 15 minutes to speak, I fasted intensely that day, as was my custom and protocol every time I would be used. When I speak, the atmosphere changed and the message was well received, I think because I was new and they hadn't seen my style of speaking before, which helped to make the message more effective.

When I get to my seat, I have a Facebook request from people in the congregation and after service, different people are asking me to help and work in their department. I remember speaking to Elder Keith, he would always give me feedback and help me to improve and work on my craft, even until this day – I am truly grateful for him and his input. He was telling me that someone said, after hearing me speak… "You can tell he's from Bethel," which made us laugh.

From that point on, I was heavily involved in church and there most if not all services. Elder Bruce was in charge of the men's department, I would spend a lot of time with him, especially praying, we would meet on Thursday at church after I finished work and pray together. The way that I prayed changed as I learned a lot from Elder Bruce, in terms of the way he prayed and the topics he would tell us to pray about. I was getting the best of both worlds, everything that I learned from Bethel and everything I was learning at New J.

Elder Bruce was also in charge of the armour bearing team, that's when you assist people, mainly preachers, before, during and after they finish preaching. In Bethel, their annual meeting was convocation at Kelvin Way, in New J, their annual meeting was LOUD conference, all the UK branches would attend, as well as churches from USA and Africa. I would be a part of the team for several years, where I would serve and help. It gave me the opportunity to be around some great men of God, one was Bishop Tudor Bismark, he is well known, been invited to speak many times at Bishop TD Jakes church, to name a few. It was a pleasure to amour bear him and listen to his stories. I would study him and how he operated as man, how he spoke and his mentality and thought process. Another Bishop was Bishop Smith who would go onto take over as the overall leader of Jabula (that's the name of the organisation). I would go on to learn a lot from him too. As time went by, I would get to amour bear Bishop Brooks on a Sunday and spend a lot of time with him and start a good personal relationship, something that I still have now and am very grateful for.

In the same year speaking for my first time at New J in 2015, Bishop Brooks had released a ten year vision for the church that God had revealed to him. Each year has a theme, the theme for 2015 was 'Building a Spiritual House'. This helped to give the church a focus for each year.

When I first joined New J and up until this point, I was very intentional of not getting close to any women, especially after my experience with Amy from PT Recruitment, I wanted to make sure that I wasn't giving anyone the wrong impression, so I just stayed clear of any women in my age group. After church services, I would greet a few people as I made my way to the door and then just leave. I just wanted to focus on God and ministry with no distractions.

As it got towards the end of 2015, I decided that I wanted to start the process of getting married, in terms of dating intentionally and purposefully. In those days, the dating world was changing, people were using social media and dating apps like Tinder, which for me was brand new and not something that I was keen on, but the more people I spoke to, the more normal I found it to be.

I started speaking to a couple of women, some were fully committed to church, whereas some just believed in God. I found the more you spoke to people, the more you found out that what they portrayed wasn't really who they were.

On these dates, I tried to be as intentional as possible and avoid any form of affection or touching, I just wanted to get to know people first. One of the best bits of advice I had from Pastor Yvette was:

"Ask question first, fall in love later."

Too many times, people including myself get this the wrong way around. We get emotionally invested, then by the time we ask questions and discover the red flags and the non-negotiables, it's too late and we're already in love knowing that the relationship is wrong and can't work. After all my mistakes in the past, I was desperate to avoid all of this.

As 2015 was coming to an end, I would continue to date and keep Pastor Yvette in the loop. In my family, however, there were big surprises ahead. Around November/December, my mom called me into a room to speak to me privately, in my head, all I was thinking was 'no good can come from this conversation'. She began to speak and say that Daddy Fletcher had been to the hospital and got some bad news, I don't remember what she said after that, all I heard was bad news. I remember maybe five years prior being at Hill Top and looking at my grandparents and realising that they wouldn't be here forever, as silly as this sounds. But I wasn't expecting this day to come so quickly. I was thinking, we can pray for healing, but eventually everyone has to die and no amount of prayer can stop that. I sat on the bed in a daze trying to come to term with the news.

But my mom had more news, she says that my cousin Shabeena is pregnant, this was a major shock to me. I had been in the hospital when she was born, I had changed her nappy, so it was difficult to hear this, in my mind, she was still my little cousin. Apparently, I was one of the people she was scared to tell.

This was a lot of information to take in all at one time. I couldn't imagine what our family would look like in the near future.

Chapter Reflections

- *Have you ever been spoken and criticised about your character/behaviour, especially when you knew everything that you heard was true? How did you respond?*
- *What are your key individual strengths and what comes naturally to you? Have you put yourself in an environment where your skills can be maximised, or are you wasting your talents?*
- *Are you now, or, when you were looking for a spouse; did/do you have a clear plan in terms of what you need and want in a spouse, with clear non-negotiables? If not, what results have you seen?*

Chapter 16
The Circle of Life

After hearing the news about Daddy Fletcher and Shabeena, I needed some time to collect my thoughts. My first response was to speak to Shabeena. I didn't like the fact that she felt awkward, especially with me about being pregnant. We had a conversation about it all and I reassured her that I didn't look at her any differently and that she didn't need to feel a way with or around me.

With the situation with Daddy Fletcher, I don't know if I was in denial or was just blocking it from my mind, but I pretty much acted like I hadn't heard anything. Afterall, what could I say or do, as I said before, we all have to die one day. In the Bible, Jesus raised Lazarus from the dead when he died from a sickness, but there would come another day where Lazarus would have to eventually die and there would be no resurrection in the same way as before. My mind was all over the place.

As I was still living at Hill Top with my grandparents, I would see Daddy Fletcher's strength and health slowly deteriorate, although he would do his best to hide this, he was a proud man in this respect.

As we entered into the new year, 2016, no one new that just a month ago that Christmas would have been our last family event together as a whole family. I'm glad I made a video that Christmas capturing everyone in the different rooms at Hill Top.

"Life is about creating and capturing memories with loved ones, we're not here long on this earth."

In January, on an ordinary week day, Daddy Fletcher went to go upstairs to bed as per usual, only on this night, he just didn't have the strength in legs to make it past the first few steps. It was past 11pm, I remember looking at the clock in the hallway as it made a ticking sound as time passed. Daddy Fletcher was the one who would always take responsibility to wind the clock up when it stopped moving, it was one of those old grandfather clocks.

Mommy Fletcher called me from my room, it was just us three in the house at this point. We both tried to support him, to help get him upstairs, but it just wasn't working. We tried for a good 25 minutes, but still nothing. The reality of my mom's words about Daddy Fletcher's health started to become a reality, only this time I couldn't choose to ignore it.

That night, Daddy Fletcher had to sleep downstairs. Either the next day or not many days later on an evening, I heard a loud thud coming from the bathroom, this time there were a lot of people in the house. We all rushed to the bathroom, Daddy Fletcher had fallen and hit his head as he fell forward. I think it was me and my aunty Sally who picked him up and tried to sit him back up. I remember Daddy Fletcher just constantly apologising and saying, "I'm sorry."

I was heartbroken, but was fighting back the tears, telling him, "it's okay, you don't need to apologise," whilst my aunty Sally was rubbing his head, looking for any visible wounds.

I'm not a mind reader, but I felt that Daddy Fletcher was ready to go, I know he wouldn't want to live a life where he couldn't do the basic things for himself, in terms of looking after himself and didn't want to be a 'burden' to others, in his own mind.

We brought him into the living room and called the rest of the family and made them aware and they came down. We had decided to call the ambulance, due to the fact that he had hit his head, he seemed fine at the time, but we didn't want to take any chances.

The ambulance turned up and took him to Sandwell hospital. From this point, things get hazy for me in terms of the sequence of events. I remember the whole family being at the hospital, I don't know how many days this was after he first went in, but I remember the doctors saying that basically there was nothing that they could do. When I heard that, I found the nearest exit and stood outside in the cold, it was freezing but my body wasn't registering the cold as my broken heart was taking precedent. I felt paralysed in this situation, I didn't know what to do. Part of me was saying to pray that he is kept alive, the other part was saying, "Pray to keep him alive for what? What standard of living would he have if he was kept alive. Plus eventually, everyone has to die and no amount of prayer can stop that."

So I just prayed in tongues, with my mind saying, "Lord, let your will be done."

"For one who speaks in a tongue speaks not to men but to God: for no one understands him, but he utters mysteries in the Spirit." 1 Corinthians 14:2 (ESV)

I remember going in to see Daddy Fletcher, his eyes were open and he was conscious, but he looked in distress. The doctor said that he wasn't in any pain. I had seen him look a similar way at his last prayer meeting not long ago. Before he had his fall at home, there was one Monday night where he couldn't make it downstairs, so we had prayer meeting in the bedroom. There's something special about that bedroom, it was also a prayer war room, filled with the daily prayers of Mommy Fletcher for decades and before that the prayers of Mama, my great grandmother.

I was asked to pray that night, there's been times where I have prayed or preached and God has entered the atmosphere and things have changed, but this night, I prayed with every fibre of my being from deep down from my soul until I could feel it in my diaphragm. When I finished, Daddy Fletcher was just looking up at the ceiling with a peaceful look on his face as though he could see something that no one else could see. This look was similar to what I saw at the hospital, as though he was at the crossroads of life and death and was about to transfer over. Looking back, it felt like that prayer was to prepare him to cross over, he just looked peaceful and was smiling.

Again, my memory is foggy with this scenario, but either that same night or the next day, they moved him to a separate ward in the hospital where he had his own room. The first night he went into the hospital, when I got back home at Hill Top, I just cried and cried. I couldn't imagine life without Daddy Fletcher, he was more than a grandad to me, he was like another father. I was in my 30s but I still called him Daddy Fletcher just like I had always done since I could talk, I spent every day at Hill Top from pre-school, infant, primary and high school, all the way through 6th form, university and to my work life and he was there every step of the way… and now he would be leaving and never coming back. This was a tough pill to swallow.

Daddy Fletcher was now in his own room on the morning of the 12th February. A phone call was made to the family that he had taken a turn for the worse and that we needed to come quickly. I remember being between Dudley

Port and Castlegate Dudley. I don't remember where I was going, I just turned the car around and raced to the hospital. When I get there, it was just my cousin Rachel and I who met at the front at the hospital or somewhere in reception, I don't remember.

We both got into the elevator to get to Daddy Fletcher's room, as we walk towards the reception to ask where to go, one of the staff said, "He's in there, he's gone."

We said, "What do you mean gone?"

She replied, "He just passed a few minutes ago peacefully."

At this point, my emotions are all over the place, one because Daddy Fletcher is now dead and secondly, I'm fuming at the manner in which the staff member communicated the information. I didn't know whether to cry or start constructing a letter of complaint.

Rachel and I walk in together and see his body on the bed, we both start crying, I go straight into the bathroom and stay there for good five minutes, I was mentally in limbo and didn't know what to do except cry. Rachel was more composed than me, I think she started calling the family and letting them know, so they wouldn't find out when they came. I was useless and like a statue.

One by one, different family members turned up, some were already aware and some weren't, I think. It was a difficult few hours and different people handled things in different ways. One of the hardest things was to see Mommy Fletcher cry, it took a while for things to sink in, she sat in the chair next to him for a while before it hit her. It was hard because there's nothing you can do or say to make things better.

After we had time to partially deal with the situation, it was time to let church leaders know and then prepare for 'nine nights', that's when people come to your house to show support and to pray with you, but you provide food and drinks – I never understood this, but it was a Jamaican tradition. After having a meeting, different duties were delegated to different people and we pulled and worked together.

Everyone's main concern was Mommy Fletcher, she had been married for more than 50 years and woke up to the same person every day and now he was gone. My mom moved into Hill Top with my brother and sister to be there for Mommy Fletcher.

The funeral date was scheduled for the next month on the 14th of March, which was also my dad's birthday. There were family that would be coming from overseas for the funeral. Mommy Fletcher's brother called Uncle Errol came with his daughter, Linda and his two grandkids, Jack and Gemma. Also, Daddy Fletcher's son, Edward came with his two sons, Carter and Darren. So there was a lot of organising and planning to do as they all either stayed at Hill Top or with Polly and Gerald. I moved out of my room and my mom, brother, sister and I stayed in Mommy Fletcher's room, it was 'cosy', but to be fair, I think having us all there helped Mommy Fletcher.

Normally in the morning, Mommy Fletcher would get up in the morning and make Daddy Fletcher a drink and some food, but now he wasn't there, so she would do it for my mom, I think after looking after her husband for all these years, it felt weird not having someone there to take care of.

During this time, I was still working from home, the company weren't that sympathetic, I think through all of this, I took one or two days off, including the day that Daddy Fletcher passed away, but my focus wasn't on work as you could imagine.

Throughout this whole process, I lost touch with some of the women I was dating, but now that we were preparing for the funeral, plus had a house full of guests, dating would be something that I wanted to do, as I was still looking to get married, but could also do with taking my mind off my current situation.

I had been talking to this woman that I met through a mutual friend called Coreene, we had mainly been texting and only spoke a few times on the phone, mostly because there was nowhere for me to go in the house for any privacy to really talk. After speaking to other women, she stuck out to me, we had the same passion for God, she had no children, which was rare to find, she came from a big family like mine, was family orientated and shared the same values as me. When I started dating, most girls didn't share the traditional values that I had seen in Mommy Fletcher and Daddy Fletcher's marriage, so when Coreene said this was important to her too, this caught my attention. I was very conscious when I was dating that I was looking for a wife for life and that this was going to be a permanent decision. I wanted someone that I was definitely physically attracted to, but I was determined not to let that be the only quality that I would take into consideration.

I arranged a date with Coreene, I wanted to have our first meet up, I didn't want to rely on photos alone as they can be deceiving. We hadn't met, but I really liked Coreene above all the other women I met.

Our first date was at Frankie & Benny's in Dudley. I wanted to have a coffee or a drink, especially as it was the first date. Imagine going on a date and you know from the very get go that you're not attracted to the person, or that for whatever reason, in your mind things would not be progressing, then you have to sit through three courses and be polite. But in the end, we had dinner at Coreene's request.

I got to the restaurant extra early, just so I could get the lay of the land and try to watch Coreene as she arrived. I needed the toilet, so had to go to the cinema across the road, the one I used to work at. During this time, Coreene arrives and messages me, she says she has arrived and is in the carpark. I make my way back over to the restaurant and wait for Coreene to walk in. As she walks in, we both try to analyse each other, how we look, how we dress, all without trying to make it obvious. We have a bit of small talk as we wait for our table. "How was your day? How long did it take you to get it here?"

When our table is ready, we are able to sit down and look properly into each other's face and talk properly. What I didn't take into consideration, was everything that I had been dealing with from work, Daddy Fletcher passing away and helping with the funeral and overseas family. I remember just feeling all my energy going. It was hard for me to talk and even smile, it felt like my entire body was crashing. Normally, on a date, I'm in great form, plus I'm a sales person, so I know how control a conversation and ask the right questions to create great conversation, but not that night. I had to excuse myself and go to the toilet, splash water on my face and try to revitalise myself. I liked what Coreene was about and didn't want to make a bad impression, because with first dates, it's make or break. As we said goodbye after the date, I had no idea of what she thought about me or the date.

After this, my focus shifted back to the upcoming funeral. I was asked to speak on behalf of all the grandchildren. If you know me, you know I don't like having to do thing at events, I would much rather relax and do nothing, but for Daddy Fletcher, I would be happy to be involved.

On the day of the funeral, everyone met at Hill Top and Uncle Errol prayed before we left. It was a nice funeral overall, from the leading, the songs and most of the tributes, I say some, because some people quite clearly came unprepared and tried to speak off the top of their head. In my opinion, unless you're a highly skilled speaker, it's best to prepare something, or at least have bullet points, to me, I find it disrespectful to do otherwise, but that's just me. The rest of the day went well and the family were largely pleased of how the day went. Now it was all about adjusting to this new normal. The family had discussions of how things would be moving forward, my mom, brother and sister were still living at Hill Top, even after our overseas family had left. A decision was in discussion for my aunty Sally's family, Marcus her husband, Shabeena and Rachel to move from their home in Darlaston into Hill Top, to live with Mommy Fletcher, but before anything would change, my mom would remain at Hill Top.

After my first date with Coreene, we were still talking, but she seemed a lot more distance. Normally, I would text her every morning which would start up a daily conversation, but time went by where we weren't speaking as much.

I don't believe God picks your spouse for you, but I do believe he'll give you hints and tips when you meet a good potential and that's what I felt about Coreene. Every morning for a season, I would have this internal battle where I would go back and forth on whether I would message her in the morning. I couldn't tell if she was properly interested in me, or if I was wasting my time. What I didn't know, was based on her past experiences with men, especially black men, she was testing me to see if I genuinely wanted her and was willingly to pursue her in the face of adversity or in this case, one-word replies. This is what she prayed to God for, so that she would be sure if I was the right guy. So everyday I'm arguing with God saying that I'm not going to text her and she can text me first for once, not knowing, God was giving me the answer and instruction to pass this test.

"We may not always understand WHY God tells us to do something, but as long as it's God's voice, just do it."

We finally get the chance to have our second date, then a couple of days prior, she cancels as 'her sister has gone into labour', I thought she was lying and using this as an excuse to cancel, but it turns out she was serious. Shortly after her sister gave birth to her first daughter, we finally go on our second date. This time I would be ready, I made sure that I went to bed early the night before so that I was fully rested. On the night of the date, as I'm about to walk out the door, my mom and sister stop me as they stand at the top of the steps, before wishing me luck.

For the second date, we went to an Italian restaurant, the date went really well, the conversation flowed nicely, it was a good atmosphere and all in all, it was a great night. I was still invoking my no touch, no affection rule when dating, especially as this was our second date, but as we leave the restaurant, it's a bit chilly, so Coreene hooks arms with me to get warm. Previously, this would have bothered me, but it felt so natural and seamless and I welcomed it. I walk her to her car and then message her later to make sure she got home safe.

At Hill Top, transition was taking place, my mom, brother and sister moved back home and I would join them, as Sally and her family moved into Hill Top. As soon as I moved home, I singlehandedly clean the entire house, in anticipation of inviting Coreene round. In the meantime, we would continue to date, going cinema, go-karting and plenty of walks in Sandwell valley park. I really enjoyed the park; this was something I took from Polly and Gerald. But it gave Coreene and I plenty of time to talk and get to know each other. I wanted to know everything that I could during the dating stage, after all, I was dating with purpose, looking for a wife. Not a woman to become a wife, but a wife with wife qualities.

"He who finds a WIFE finds a good thing and obtain favour from the LORD."
Proverbs 18:22 (ESV)

I know some people look for a spouse, thinking they can change the person or mould them into their ideal image of a husband or wife, but I decided to find someone who already had the qualities that I was looking for, from the list I made in 2009 when Bishop Brooks told me to make a plan for my entire life.

When getting to know Coreene, I asked her about her early childhood memories and key events that she deemed important in her life, to help try and understand her 'whoness', as Bishop Brooks would say. Whilst it was fun getting to know her, I was still very much focused on seeing if we have the same vision for what married life looks like. The more I got to know Coreene, was the more and more sure I was that I wanted her for my wife. It was like my spirit could see who she really was, or the person that God had created her to be. My mind couldn't see it and it was in no way observable to any other part of me, but I knew something was there. This was the first time that I was in a relationship that was right, and it gave me peace, no guilt or shame like in the past, in fact this was the opposite, God would be pleased with this relationship. It was around this time that I had a vision or daydream of the future, it was Coreene on a hospital bed holding our child, the image was detailed, the maternity gown, even down to the hairstyle, but I kept this to myself. All I knew was that Coreene was the woman for me, she was beautiful inside and out. Even down to the meaning of her name was a sign to me. When I was dating, I had certain things that I wanted in my wife, a big part of that was the whole traditional household, in terms of a man doing certain things and a woman doing certain things. Some people told me that I would never find that in this day and age and women like that don't exist and that no woman wants to serve their husband like the wives of our grandparent's generation. But on our second date, I asked Coreene what her name meant and she said 'servant' and then she added how she likes to serve and can't wait to get married and take care of her husband. All this was a sign to me.

A couple months after Coreene's niece was born in March, Shabeena gave birth to her son Ethan, his birthday was a day after Coreene's, 27th May. Shabeena asked me to be Godfather, it felt like Ethan was my son and I would treat him as such, especially as he was my first Godchild.

Ethan's birth completed the circle of life in our family. It seemed like a pattern, that one generation would go and within 12 months, another generation would be born. In the year that my great grandfather died, I was born and I was the of a new generation – the great grandchildren (at that time) and in the same manner, Daddy Fletcher passed away (the great grandfather) and within 12 months another generation was born, Ethan was the first of the great grandchildren... The circle of life.

Coreene and I continued to date, I was ready to be official and exclusive with her alone, but there were some roadblocks ahead...

Chapter Reflections

- *When was the first time that a loved one passed away and how did you cope?*
- *When there's a family crisis, what role do you usually play?*
- *What are your thoughts on death and do these thoughts impact the way you live your life?*
- *Are you currently married/in a relationship? If so, how did you meet and what was your first date like?*

Chapter 17
Will You Be My Wifey? Say You'll Be My Wifey

At this stage of my life, most things seemed brand new, I had just moved back home after living at Hill Top for seven years, Daddy Fletcher had recently passed away and it was weird going to Hill Top and not seeing him there, sitting in his favourite seat and I was also dating Coreene and still in the early stages. It was like a new life.

Coreene and I continued to date and we spent more and more time together. For me, I had enough information to decide that I wanted to get more serious with her and date her exclusively, by this time, we had been dating for several months and had been on plenty of dates. In the background, I had different mentors to guide me as I was dating.

I arranged another date at a restaurant in Bentley Bridge, I was ready to speak to Coreene and state my intentions. We get to the restaurant, and I believe we ordered some drinks to start out. I remember feeling nervous, because although we had dated for a while, I wasn't sure if she was ready to get more serious, but I wouldn't let this stop me doing what I came to do.

I start speaking and explain how much I had enjoyed the past few months getting to know her, I remind her that I was wasn't just dating for dating's sake, but that I was looking for a wife and I believed that she was the one for me. I told her that I wanted us to only date each other exclusively with a plan to build upon our foundation. As I'm speaking, Coreene has a poker face, I have no idea what she is thinking or feeling. Once I finish, she would then reveal her thoughts. She starts out by saying that she too enjoyed the past few months getting to know me amongst other positive things. It felt like I was on the X-Factor show, when they get to the judge's house and the judge is about to tell them if they will be going through to the live shows. My heart is pounding and I'm nervous, I'm half listening and half zoning out, watching her lips move, almost trying to get the gist of what she is saying by the movement of lips before the sound hits my ears.

As she is speaking, she finally gets to the important bit, she says that she just wants to be friends and doesn't want things to move, at this point, every word coming out of her mouth felt like a bullet being fired from a sawed-off shotgun right into my heart. I was devasted, but tried to keep my composure as best as I could, by nodding and smiling as she was speaking. Once she finished speaking, in my mind there was no need for me to be there, I signalled the waitress and asked for the bill. As we get outside, Coreene gives me a hug, but it definitely felt like 'goodbye, have a nice life' hug, like we would never see each other again. We walk our separate ways and I go into my car, where I could take off my mask with the fake smile I had on in the restaurant whilst Coreene was talking. I was upset, Coreene was the first woman that I had pursued, all other relationships kind of just happened mutually or the woman approached me. With Coreene, I messaged her every morning, every day, even when it felt like she was interested. I was upset with God, although I was never told this was my wife, I definitely had the signs for a strong potential, and I had many times ignored my own gut feelings to follow God's instructions and now it was all for nothing.

When I get home, I delete Coreene's number out of anger and just in case I got emotional or vulnerable and would text her in my weakness, I was done.

A few days go by and out of nowhere, Coreene messages me, she had never been the first to do this before. We start speaking and she asks to meet up to talk. When we meet, she opens up to me and tells me where's she is at mentally and emotionally when it comes to dating and the future. As she is talking, things start to make a lot of sense to me, in terms of things I was wrestling with God about doing. She said that she was praying and knows the decision that she made at the restaurant was the wrong one and that she too wanted to be exclusive. We talked more about private and intimate things regarding relationships and expectations, then we officially became exclusive, I was over the moon.

Once we became exclusive, the next stage would be to meet each other's parents and family. I arranged a meal for my mom, Coreene and I to attend, it was the same restaurant that we went to on our second date. On the day, I don't know why, but I was really nervous, more than Coreene, if anything she should have been the nervous one. I guess I was hoping that they would get on and that my mom and family would approve. The meal went well, I was happy with how they both interacted and they seemed to like each other.

Next it was my turn, Coreene's parents invited me round to their house for Sunday dinner after church. That Sunday I would attend Coreene's church before going to her parent's house, again, I was so nervous. After the church service was over, I briefly met them, but the real introductions would be at the house. I also met Coreene's pastor as well as most of the church members, they were all really friendly and made me feel welcome.

After leaving the church, I made my way down to Coreene's house. I arrived early, Coreene's dad was musician and part of the worship team, so had things to do after the church service, so arrived back after me. Coreene and her mom were upstairs changing out of their church clothes whilst I waited. It felt like I was waiting to be interviewed. When Coreene's dad arrived, we spoke and got to know each other. We spoke about our families, background and church mostly whilst the ladies were preparing dinner. I enjoyed dinner, it was the four of us around the dinner table in the conservatory. It felt really natural, Coreene's dad was more talkative than her mom, I guess they were both analysing me in their own way. Coreene had two other sisters, she was the middle child. Her younger sister Linda was already married to her husband Dre and had flown the next two years prior and now had their first child. Tamina was the older sister, she was in a serious relationship with Kevin, who she would shortly go on to marry, so it looked like I would be the one to fully empty the nest.

After meeting Coreene's parents, it made me feel good and at peace that she came from a good family. This was the first time that I was in a relationship where I had peace instead of guilt or shame because of being with the wrong person for me. I loved this feeling. Around this time, we got introduced to each other's family, Coreene came to my church and then to Hill Top to meet the family, I would then go on to meet her sisters and their partners and I even went to London to meet some of Coreene's aunties and uncle. I met her aunty Ruby, who was like a second mother to her and her uncle Tom and his wife. We were in a great place and both got on well with each other's family.

We were both on the same page in terms of not wanting to date for a long time and get married, we spoke about things, but nothing was decided in terms of dates and timescales, but everything was going great, or so we thought…

With everything that had happened in the previous months, with the funeral, moving house and dating Coreene, my focus wasn't 100% at work. The role that I had was a start-up role, to build things from scratch, which started off well up until all the bad news the year before. Things at work started to get more difficult in terms of results and because I was in my probation period, they let me go. I was gutted, not because of losing this job, but because I had been let go from my two previous roles, this really affected my confidence, plus I was at a place where I was thinking about getting married and started a new life, but now I had no job.

I decided that I would use this occasion to forever get out of the recruitment industry, it wasn't something that I enjoyed, it was something that I fell into after Appco and didn't know where else to turn. I remember organising a meeting with Pastor Yvette for some guidance because I didn't know what to do with my life career wise. At this meeting, similar to what Bishop Brooks told me to do in 2009, she said to make a plan, but to look at my life and identify the things that I like to do and where I have found success in life, by looking at my entire life, even going back to schools days and school subjects. So I bought another book and created a plan and mapped everything out. I was looking into a course where I could become a teacher and get paid as well as get my qualifications at the same time, although I wasn't 100% in love with dealing with kids every day.

I was also speaking to Elder Bruce about my current work predicament, he mentioned there was a guy in church called Duane who was a manager at BT and said they were hiring. He told me to forward my CV to him and he would pass it on. I had no idea what the role was, I just wanted a job. Not long after, one day I was at home chilling when I got a call from a manager from BT, he asked if I would be available for an interview in the morning, the job was based in Solihull, right by Birmingham airport, but I didn't care.

The next day, I arrive at the BT offices and sit in the reception area where there were some other candidates. Everyone started talking about the previous interview process they had to complete online, I had no idea what they were talking about. I would come to find out that there was a whole process to get through to even get a face-to-face interview that I had apparently skipped. I'm not sure if this was down to my New J connection Duane or for another reason.

At the start of the interview, they took us all into room, there were about eight of us candidates and about seven managers in the room. They announced that this was an interview day and would consist of three stages, a group presentation, role play and then a final interview, when I heard this, my heart sunk. I started to feel nervous like I did when I was at church and thought of having to present in front of a room of people didn't sit well with me.

As we continued with the first phase, the presentation, I was happy for the 'know-it-alls' in my group to take the lead. After the presentation, the managers start firing questions at us, I suppose it was to see how we responded under pressure and to see how we could sell their products. It went well enough and I held my own when questions were fired my way.

The next stage was the role play, they leave you in a small room with 20 minutes to read a brief and prepare for a mock meeting with a potential client. Out of the six managers, for the role play, I had a guy called Ricky and there was another guy from a different part of the business. I did pretty well in the role play and met their expectations.

The last stage was the final interview where they go through your CV to learn more about your experiences. I had this woman who was one of the managers for my interview. She really took to me from the start and when we got to Appco on my CV, she was really impressed with what I had achieved as she was well acquainted with these types of organisations and knew how hard the roles were. As we finished the interview and she escorted me back to the main room, she said, "You will like working here," indicating that I had the job, but I would wait for the confirmation. Later that day, I got a call informing me that I got the job, I was over the moon, now I could start planning my future. When I was in recruitment, I never got any commission, but at BT I would be earning commission from day one even without me doing any sales, I was so grateful to God.

Because of my experience with my past two roles and them not working out, this was in my subconscious and would drive me to perform and consistently hit my targets. In my first month, I would beat everyone in the office, despite my little experience. I was working hard, because in the back of my mind was the reminder that I got let go from previous roles, so success at BT was the only option. This was perfect, because the more I performed, was the more money I made. I finally had a job that matched everything that I was taught from a young boy – the harder you work, the more you get. I started working at BT in September 2016.

For the next few months, I worked hard like crazy, I didn't really mix with anyone, I was on a mission. During this time, Coreene and I were doing great, still dating and getting to know each other and each other's family. We were growing as a couple but also as individuals, both of were changing for the better to be a better partner for the other. It wasn't easy and plain sailing, it was work, but anything in life that's worth having, always comes with hard work.

As I was settling into my job, I was now ready to progress my relationship with Coreene, I wanted us to start preparing for pre-engagement and pre-marital counselling. We spoke about getting engaged, I wanted to make sure that Coreene was ready before proposing. It was around this time that Coreene's sister got engaged too, I knew Coreene didn't want to get engaged at the same time as her sister, so I had that in mind. We knew we would be getting engaged but the time would be down to me.

In December of that year, I called a meeting with Coreene where we could properly speak and plan our future. We spoke about wedding dates and from there we could work backwards to determine how much money we would need to save each month. Originally, the date we chose was 25th August 2018, depending on if we could get the church and reception venue booked on the same day. We spoke about where to live, we both had the same areas in mind, but I was adamant that we would buy a house. It didn't make sense to me to spend thousands of pounds on the wedding and then to rent, I mean, each to their own, but that wasn't my vision for my family.

From that meeting, we bought two books, one was a wedding book for us to put all our plans in, the other was a house book, to put all our plans in. The process from here to the wedding day would be saturated with prayer and fasting and it was needed! Coreene said all the plans felt like a lot, but I said I would step in and run with things whenever she felt overwhelmed. The plan was to save for a house for all of 2017 and we would start looking for a house in 2018 only, so that we could solely focus on everything relating to the wedding plans. Because we're fasting and praying, I'm getting guidance from God of how and when to do things, something people wouldn't know this unless you knew me personally. But if you didn't know me that well, you would think I was crazy, over-ambitious, doing too much or destined for failure; Coreene and I would hear this all the way through our process, but it brought us closer together as a couple and closer to God.

As we entered 2017, we were ready with our plans, the only thing missing was my proposal. From previous dates with Coreene, I had already found out what type of ring she would like and the style. It was just down to me to speak to her dad and work out how I was actually going to propose. I got on pretty well with Coreene's dad, so I couldn't imagine him having a problem with me marrying her, plus I knew that he wanted to see all of his daughters married and happy. So I would plan and organise speaking to her dad and my proposal simultaneously.

For the engagement, in my head, I couldn't think of anywhere better than Marco Pierre White in the Mailbox in Birmingham city centre. Originally, I was looking to hire a private room where you can hold 50 people, but that wouldn't really work as we both had big families and most of Coreene's family were based in London. Besides, after thinking about this, Coreene would have liked something more private and intimate, so I arranged for a dinner table and I would propose there. I went to the restaurant one of the days after work and got a tour to become familiar with the venue and make sure that I felt comfortable with everything. I would play it off and tell Coreene that we are going for drinks and would 'see' if they happened to have any tables available. Additionally, I spoke to my friend Mikey at church and asked if he would take photos as I wanted to capture the moment. Everything was set.

Coreene's dad had been really busy with work and doing shifts, so it took longer than expected to get the chance to sit down and speak with him. It was a Monday night, Coreene was out doing her hair, so I knew she would be out for most of the evening. I even googled 'how to ask your girlfriend's father for her hand in marriage', this had to be perfect.

On the Monday night, I arrive at the house with my planning book. I wanted to show Coreene's dad, that I was serious about marrying his daughter, but also how I would do this to alleviate any concerns that he may have. The only thing missing from my presentation was a projector and a laser pen. After I finish explaining my feeling, plans and intentions for his daughter, I ask for his blessings and he was more than happy to give that to me. He wanted us to get married sooner than the date we had in mind, which made me happy, but I explained our timeline. Coreene's mom was upstairs and I asked Coreene's dad's permission to also speak with her. When Coreene's mom, entered the room she had already put two and two together. She wasn't as excited as Peter, at the time I didn't get it, but looking back I think it was because Linda had left two years prior, Tamina was already engaged and would be leaving in nine months and then Coreene would be leaving the year after and she was losing all of her girls, so now it makes sense. Obviously, I'm not a mother, but I imagine this transition would be hard on any mother. Even my own mom felt the same, she kept talking about how she would be losing me too. But at this moment, all of that didn't matter, I had just been given the green light and I was excited.

On the day of the proposal, I had my outfit ready from earlier on that day, fresh haircut and shave, I was ready! That whole week, I had practiced what I wanted to say to Coreene when I actually proposed. I had Mikey meeting me there to take the photos when we were officially engaged.

I pick up Coreene from her house, as far as she was aware, it was just another date. In the car, we have small talk, but I'm half listening and half trying to remember my lines. As we park up at the red cage carpark by the mailbox, Mikey texts me saying he is already there, I ask him to hide until the right time. I make sure to put the engagement ring on the opposite side of where Coreene is walking so there's no chance of her noticing the bulge of the ring box.

As we enter the restaurant, it's extremely noisy and our table looks really close to the neighbouring customer's table. When I came before, it was when the restaurant was fully closed, so I never got to take all of this into account – the noise and close proximity. I proceed with the plan initially, I go over and 'see' if there are any spare tables and it just so happens that the best table in the restaurant just happens to be available. When we sit down, I don't feel comfortable, I feel like I have to raise my voice to speak to Coreene, so that she could hear me, this was no place to propose. I get up and go to the 'bathroom'. I use this as an opportunity to speak to the manager who I had spoken to when I originally came before when it was quiet. I ask if there is somewhere that I can borrow to propose and then we would go back to our seats. She shows me into one of the rooms I was originally going to hire, it's perfect, we have the skyline view, the room is empty and has a nice piano in the background, it's still a bit loud, but this will more than do.

I come out the room and tell Mikey to get ready and go in the room. All I have to do now is get Coreene. As I go back to the table and try to get Coreene into the other room without raising any suspicions, I tell her we now have a better table. But Coreene being Coreene doesn't want to move as she loves the spot we have. I'm like, "Trust me, this one is better," Coreene still isn't convinced, so I take charge and take her coat and take her by the hand. We walk in to the room and she sees Mikey and asks why he is there, I take her by the hand and begin to speak, what I didn't know was that because of the background noise from the restaurant, Coreene didn't hear all of what I said but got the general message. As I'm talking, she starts shaking and tears began to flow and then I ask her, "Will you marry me?" aka, will you be wifey? Say you'll be my wifey.

Chapter Reflections

- *Are you in a relationship? If so, what are some of your fondest memories from the beginning of your relationship?*
- *Are you married or engaged? If so, why did you propose or accept the proposal?*

Chapter 18
Engagement Ring to the Wedding Ring

As I am down on bended knee looking into Coreene's tearful eyes, I wait for her response. As she regains her composure amidst all the excitement and shock, she says, "Yes." I can't describe the feeling that I had in that moment and for rest the of the evening. It's a feeling that I have only felt at key moments in my life, receiving the gift of the Holy Spirit, passing my driving test and then getting my first car and getting promoted at different stages of my life. It was a feeling that signified a new chapter in my life and going to another level.

We were both so excited that when we went back to our seats, we lost our appetite. Before announcing on social media, we told our families first. I was on cloud nine and couldn't wait to move from the engagement ring to the wedding ring, but there were 16 months in between. For the next few weeks, my favourite line was, "I have a fiancé." I would be upstairs in my room and call my sister from downstairs, when she came into the room, I would say, "I have a fiancé," and then dismiss her. I would call family members on the phone just to say, "I have a fiancé," and then hang up, I couldn't contain how happy I was.

One thing I did learn at this stage in my life was that, not everybody will be happy for you or celebrate with you. I found that sometimes people can only be happy for you when they are happy. So if you got a new car, some people can only be happy if their car is new; if you're expecting a baby, some people can only be happy for you if they're pregnant too. This was a steep learning curve for me because I had no problem being happy for people even if they had what I wanted, but not everyone thinks that way. Over the next 16 months, I would learn to smile at people whenever I heard negativity without responding in the manner that I wanted to – more character development.

Soon after our engagement, I would start my character development training. I had people telling me that I got engaged too soon and if I were to ask their advice, they would have told me not to do it. This is why my relationship with God is the best thing in my life, because when I pray and get guidance from Him, it doesn't matter what other people say to me. Some of my relationships began to change, this was something that I was warned about by Dre and Kevin based on their experiences. They said people will change and act funny with you, but it comes with the territory.

Once everyone knew we were engaged, people began to ask where we were going to live and when we said we were going to buy a house, some people looked at us like we were crazy. They would say, "How are you going to get married and buy a house at the same time?"

"Planning a wedding is stressful by itself and buying a house by itself is stressful, so how are you going to do both at the same time?" Then when we said we would only start looking for house next year January 2018, eight months before the wedding, it was like throwing gasoline on a fire. Many people in our circle were either renting or when they got married, or they did the wedding first and then years later got the house. But what people didn't see and know was the prayer and fasting behind the scenes and the instruction I was getting from God. Had I not known God, I would have probably listened to everyone's 'sound advice' and changed the plans, but God!

I felt a bit of pressure, because this was the first time that I was becoming the man of my own family and I was responsible for my future wife, and I wanted to look after her and give her everything. Now the buck stopped with me.

I remember having a meeting with Coreene shortly after our engagement to go over our plans again. I explained to her that the next 16 months would be tight based on our plans, but after the wedding day we would live our best lives. At the time, my car was all raggedy and could have done with changing, but I stayed true to the plan and vision. We set goals for after the wedding day, we said we would go on holiday at least four times within our first 18 months of marriage as a means to build a strong foundation before having kids. We also set goals for new cars too. For the next 16 months, I would watch people around me get new cars, buy new clothes and go on holiday, but it didn't faze me one bit, but that wasn't my season; my season would come after the wedding the day and because I knew that and understood the seasons of my life, I could be happy for other people and celebrate their wins with them.

So now it was time to plan the wedding, we pulled out the wedding book and looked at each part, churches, wedding receptions, bridal party, cars and so on.

This process helped Coreene and I get to know each other better and also test us both in terms of working together and agreeing and compromising. By the end, we were better communicators. During this process we disagreed more than ever and with the pressure of all the wedding planning, this intensified everything. This made me fearful, because growing up I had never seen my parents argue, they would always do it privately, I assume. So whenever I was in relationship, especially now, I always felt like there was something wrong with the relationship. Thankfully, we were still going to pre-marital counselling, and I learned that arguments are healthy, when done in the right way and the real thing to be concerned about is when both people stop arguing, that means they both have given up and stop caring.

"Counselling is key and definitely needed."

At work, everything was going extremely well, I was in a role where I was earning commission every month and some months there were extra bonuses. God was really blessing me and helping me through this process.

At church that year, I had the opportunity to preach on a Sunday morning at New J, the theme that year was 'Building Assets' and my topic was 'Loose Your Mind'. It was a great word that I got from God and I was reasonably pleased with the delivery. I was and am still perfecting my craft. That was the first time Coreene had seen me speak. I remember going over to her after the service and her looked at me in a way that she had never done before, a look of shock I remember. When we were dating, I never really showed her my gifting. I know in church, especially with some women, they like the 'idea' of being married to a preacher or a musician, so I took that out of the equation.

By this time, we were in the middle of our wedding plans. We had booked the church, it was a church that Coreene had chosen years ago, it was really big inside and very bright and beautiful, it even matched our wedding colour scheme. The reverend was a nice guy and we got on really well too. We had gone back and forth on venues for the reception and ended up with Walsall football stadium. Neither of us were head over heels with this as a reception venue, but because of the date of the wedding, a lot of other venues were already booked. With this venue, we had to sort our own caterer, tablecloths, cutlery, centre pieces, decorations and practically everything else.

The next thing we secured was the car for the bridesmaids and then the photographer. We both decided on a guy called Benjamin, we had a list of 10 photographers and/or videographers. When we met Benjamin, we both chose him. He was a really nice guy and how he worked made you feel like he really cared about our wedding day. He had a package that was far more competitive than everyone else's and he offered more. His package included an engagement photoshoot, he would hire out space at a hotel and we would take pictures and go on to use one for our 'Save The Date' flyer. We both really enjoyed that day, the colour scheme was black and gold and we both got dressed up in formal wear. At the hotel, everyone was watching us, trying to work out who we were, it was an amazing day and the pictures came out perfect – we had chosen the right man.

Everything was going pretty well at this time in terms of work, church and the wedding plans, I remember going to my local KFC and seeing one of the guys from New J's youth working there, I even got some free KFC… everything was great (remember this point for later).

As the year progressed, we arrived at Tamina and Kevin's wedding day in September. Coreene was a chief bridesmaid and I was an Usher. On the day I was almost analysing everything, trying to learn and pick up tips that would help me for my wedding. When we get to the reception, I tell Coreene that I don't want to give a speech, I still had a thing where I got really nervous, and I just wanted to relax. But during the reception Coreene said that master of ceremonies would call me regardless. When I got that text, my belly instantly started doing summersaults. I was extremely nervous and was about to vomit. I had to leave the room and go outside for some fresh air, but it didn't help my nerves. I was taking deep breaths and trying to compose myself, but the nerves got the better of me. At one point, I cover my mouth as I feel the vomit starting to rise up in me, it felt like the old days at church. Thankfully, nothing came out and I finally was able to regain my composure just before I was called to speak. I think people thought that I just never wanted to speak and thought I was being rude, but they didn't know the usual process that I go through when I have to speak publicly. To this day people don't believe me when I say I get nervous when I speak and sometimes vomit.

The speech went really well and was well received, I had a few people come up to me and compliment me. In the end, I was glad I did it.

"Adversity shows a man to himself." Albert Einstein.

Once Tamina and Kevin's wedding was over, Coreene and I could move forward with our wedding plans. Because we were engaged at the same and Tamina was getting married first, Coreene wanted us to just plan in the background, as this time was Tamina's. So we never really spoke about or did things around Coreene's family during this time. We waited a month after Tamina's wedding before releasing our 'Save The Date' flyers to our family and friends. That was an exciting time for us and especially Coreene. Now things seem to feel even more real.

As the year of 2017 was winding down, Coreene's church had a function at a venue called WS10 Banqueting Suite in Wednesbury. At the event, Coreene raised the suggestion of having our wedding reception here, it was a venue that her family liked too. With the venue, they provided everything, food, decorations, centre pieces if you wanted; even the food was unlimited and people wouldn't have to leave their seats and this would help drastically with our plans and take away pressure and stress. In the end, we arrange a meeting with the manager, who's a great guy, known by some of my family and friends, and we book our reception. I was just glad to have one more thing to tick off the list.

As we enter in December's Christmas break, Coreene and I are where we planned to be. The original goal was to look for a house starting in January 2018, but I said to Coreene that we should start the process now because we're off over Christmas, so we can view more houses in this time frame, rather than in a normal week, where we would have to go to work and then go to view houses. Coreene wanted to take a break, to be fair, the whole year was pretty intense with all the wedding planning and counselling, on top of normal life. But I said, if we do this now, this will set us up for our future, I could just feel it. In the end, Coreene got on the same page as me.

Neither of us had purchased a house before or knew the procedure, so I arranged time with people that I knew purchased a house recently to get as much advice as possible. The next thing was decide what our limit was, in terms of the maximum price for a house. Again, neither of us had a clue what to set as the maximum. This is where prayer and fasting was key. I prayed to God and asked him for my limit and he said £'X' amount is my limit. When I hear this at the start of the process, I was like, "Okay, God, no problem," but at that time, I didn't know if that was a 'good amount' or not. When we start looking and viewing properties, my first reaction was "God, this isn't enough to get a decent house." I remember praying and pleading with God for permission to add at least another

£20K, but He never gave me permission to do this. Because of my history and relationship with God, I wouldn't dare step out of his will or his instruction to me. So I tried to get clever and spoke to my mom and said, "Have you ever prayed to God about something, you heard an answer but you're not sure if it was God," my mom looked at me and said, "James, you know God's voice, if you heard, then you know if it's Him or not." After, that, I would be totally submitted to the budget that God gave to me and would not question Him again.

We viewed our first property on 26th December, 10 days later we had viewed our 19th property, there was one more on the list, but we wanted the 19th one. We sat in the car and prayed together for this house, what we didn't know, was that God was saying, "Nah, bigger."

"Now to Him [God] who is able to do far more abundantly than all we ask or think…" Ephesians 3:20

After viewing the 19th house, we had an hour or so until our scheduled appointment to view the 20th and last house. We went to McDonalds to get a drink while we waited, in our minds all we wanted was the 19th house, to the point where we were considering not going, thank God we did.

As we arrive at the 20th house, we both like the house from the outside. That day the estate agent was sick, so it would be the owners that would meet us and show us around. It was a married couple, I would say they were in their late 60s/early 70s, they were a lovely couple, Sally and John. Sally had grown up in the house with her mom and family, until she left and got married. Her mom lived there until she passed away, after which Sally rented it out, which didn't go so well, so she had decided to sell it.

As we went into the house and walked through the front door, there was no carpet, they had done quite a bit of work on the house in terms of improving the structure, which gave me confidence. Coreene and Sally walked around together, while John and I walked around together. I loved the house and could see us living there. John and I walked into the living room towards the back that lead to the garden, the blinds were shut, so I peeked through to take a look at the garden. As I looked out, I noticed there was no fence to separate our garden from the neighbour's garden. I asked John about this, he said there was no fence and all of the space was one garden for the house, I couldn't believe it, it was absolutely massive, I was sold!

Coreene was still walking around with Sally, but she loved it too. On top of that, the house was a two-minute drive from my mom's house and an eight-minute drive from Coreene's parents house, it was perfect.

Sally and John gave us some time to speak properly, we both were in agreement, we had to have this house. That day was perfect, because the estate agent wasn't there, it gave us the chance to speak to the owners before making an offer, so they knew who we were. As we all stood in the living room, I make this 'Martin Luther King – I have a dream speech' to them both. The price they wanted was more than the budget that God had given me and I was honest and upfront about that in my speech. After that, we all leave, I go back home round the corner and I immediately put my offer in. Within 30 minutes, I get a call to say that our offer was accepted!

"Little is much, when God is in it!"

I can't dance, but when I got that phone call, I started dancing. From the day we put the offer in, to the day we had the keys in our hand, was 49 days! Without weekends, 35 days! You have to remember, we were told this wasn't possible, it's too much to do, "what if it takes months for the house to complete," don't get your hopes up etc… BUT GOD! I knew God would do it, but the manner and the speed in which He did it, blew us and everyone around us away.

"Come on God, now you're just showing off, lol."
– James Beckford

During this process, I had people sow words of doubt into my spirit, to the point where my spirit was crushed and I questioned God's word. I had to go on fasting to pull myself together and scrape other people's words and negativity out of my spirit. That's why it's best not to tell certain people what your next move is, because they can end up killing your dream/vision.

When we got the keys to the house, we set up some chairs in the middle of the living room and we prayed and thanked God for what he had done. We were growing together as a couple in God. Once we got the house, not only did God bless us, but it would turn out to be a blessing and inspiration to other people. Following this, a few people from our families and friends would now go on to start the process to purchase a house. The thing that was thought of as impossible, was now possible, not only to us, but to others.

After we got the house, for me everything would be smooth sailing, as in my mind, the most important thing was having somewhere to live, as opposed to spending loads of money on a wedding day.

We spent some time doing work on the house and getting some basic things in. We got the keys in February, but I never moved in until June. After that point, Coreene would come round every day after work, but she would leave by 10pm. Now that we had our house, we wanted even more to be married there and then, but we would need to wait.

As the year went on leading up to the wedding, Aiden, my best man had organised a stag do to Marbella. This came at the right time as it gave me time to switch off from planning. I was very grateful for this, not only did Aiden organise everything before and during the stag do, but he also paid for my ticket and room.

But what happens in Marbella, stays in Marbella! When I got back, I had another one for those who didn't go to Marbella, it was nice to have a night out and just chill.

After I came back from my stag do, the countdown was on and we were in within touching distance of the wedding day. We had continued our pre-marital counselling sessions with New J. Coreene wanted us to also have a session with her Pastor, so we arranged a session. It was really good, it helped her Pastor to get to know me a bit better and make her feel comfortable, knowing that Coreene would be in safe hands. At the end of the meeting, she asked if I could preach at her church for Father's Day. I said I would speak to my Pastor and get permission first before accepting. Bishop Brooks knew Coreene's pastor and was happy for me to go. I spoke '10 Points of a Real Man'. As per usual, I would pray and fast and let God give me a word, then I would copy and paste on the day, it was a good service.

As we were almost at the wedding day, we were still experiencing people having something to say about the way we planned things. You would have thought after people had seen what God had done for us with the house and all the plans so far, that we knew what we were doing under God's leadership. But people have always got something to say, no matter what you do, so you may as well just live your life and that's exactly what we did.

One of the last things we did as part of our counselling was attend a church retreat weekend, it was one of the best things we did as a couple. It was really in depth and intense and was definitely needed. It helps couples to really speak and address things that have either been ignored or just not thought of. Coreene and I found it so useful and we were both glad we invested this time into our relationship.

The week of the wedding, I booked Coreene and I into a very much needed spa day. We felt so relaxed and could for once take our minds off the wedding. The day before the wedding, we were finalising the last bits and bobs. I was so busy that I never had chance to practice my wedding speech and by the time I got home, I was so tired that I never got chance to really go over things. Knowing that I probably wouldn't sleep properly anyway, I went to bed to get as much sleep as possible, ready for the big day, where Coreene and I would go from the engagement ring to the wedding ring, and she would finally be my wife!

<u>Chapter Reflections</u>

- *Have you ever had some good news or success, but you noticed that certain people were not happy for you? How did you handle this?*
- *Have you ever had big plans/goals and then had people tell you that they're not possible? How did you respond?*

Chapter 19
Two Become One

August 31st, 2018, the day that I had been waiting for was finally here. I remember waking up that morning and crying, it was a mixture of emotion, I was upset that Daddy Fletcher wasn't here, I know he would have loved to be here. The other reason why I was crying was because of everything that God had done for Coreene and I since the day I met her.

"If it had not been the LORD who was on our side…" Psalms 124:2

On top of that, I was grateful for everyone in my family who helped me along the way to make my journey easier. Many of my aunties, my parents and grandparents reached out to me and helped me in various ways and this brought tears to my eyes.

I got up and got showered and went for a walk in the garden, it was a beautiful hot summers day, just gorgeous, it was perfect. The plan was for the groom men and best men to arrive at my house in the morning, where the camera man would come to take some shots of us.

As I'm slowing walking around the garden, mentally preparing myself for the day ahead and praying, I get a phone call from Benjamin, the photographer, he had someone working with him that day for the videoing aspect. He's on the phone breathing heavy and panicking, he says his car is not working, he's tried various things and that he's waiting for the garage to open to take his car. He would need his car to get to my house, then to Coreene's parents and for the rest of the day. I interject as he is explaining, "Benjamin, calm down, it's okay. Forget your car, get a taxi and just get here now, I'll pay for it and I'll organise your transport for the day." He starts to calm down and is grateful. I was thinking that I needed people to help keep me calm, never mind me taking care of other people. After I put the phone down, I call my dad and explain the situation and ask for his help and for him to come to my house and of course he is happy to help for the day – I was extremely grateful towards and for my dad, he just stepped in and helped out for the whole day, no questions asked.

The groomsmen arrive at my house and start to get ready, we had to wait until Benjamin arrived to get fully dressed to capture the moment. Once we get dressed, we went into the garden for some pictures, it was at this moment that things started to feel very real and my nerves kick in again, up until the wedding I would take massive deep breaths to try and calm myself down.

The morning flew by, before I knew it, it was time to leave and get to the church. There was a bit of traffic which never helped my nerves. When we get to the church, it's pretty much full and 90% of our guests had arrived. Everything looked beautiful. I was greeting people and thanking them for coming as I walked down the aisle to the front, my nerves were very, very strong. The worship team and musicians from my church were providing the music that day. Coreene's car was stuck in traffic so the worship team started some songs whilst people were waiting. As soon as they started, all my nerves went! I went from nervous to fully confident, the atmosphere had changed.

Coreene and the bridesmaids finally arrive and now the ceremony starts, I was so happy and excited. The bridesmaids walked down with their paired groomsmen and everyone looks great, the music is on point, it's all good. Finally, they play the bride's song to walk down to, it's by an artist called Major and titled 'Why I Love You'. Before I met Coreene, I hadn't heard of this song and had other songs in mind, by when she introduced the song to me, I instantly fell in love with it.

Coreene is escorted down the aisle by her father, who then gives her away. I remember Coreene just looking straight ahead when she first arrived at the altar, her nerves were going too. The ceremony seemed to go pretty quickly, I remember saying my vows and placing the ring on Coreene's finger. Throughout the ceremony, the worship team and musicians were spectacular, there was a real atmosphere there that day. People even came off the street into the church, like a scene from the film Sister Act because of the music. Even my work colleagues who weren't church goers commented about how good the 'band' were.

One of the songs that we requested was 'You Made a Way' by Travis Greene, because that's exactly what God kept doing for us. The song was led by one of the young guys on the worship team named Darrell. At this point, he was currently dating my sister. Do you remember that time that I got free food from KFC, he was the guy that sorted me out... It all makes sense now, he was buttering me up lol. Last year September, there was a wedding anniversary and most of the church were there, I noticed my sister and Darrell sitting together all night giggling, but I thought nothing of it.

Anyway, Darrell and the worship team nailed the song and had me in tears, the words from the verses and chorus were very real to me. I remember being at the altar with Coreene thinking that all the planning that we had done for the past 18 months was now over. Every time we got paid, all the money went towards the wedding or the house, but now we could actually live our lives and not think about planning, a huge weight was lifted, this was another huge LCI (Life changing Incident) and my life would never be the same again, because now, two had become one!

"That is why a man leaves his father and mother and is united to his wife, and they become one flesh." Genesis 2:24

At the end of the ceremony, the Reverend presented for the first time Mr and Mrs Beckford, we exited the church, where we took some more photos, before we both got into our limo. We could finally breathe for a little while. After taking photos at Wolverhampton Park, we arrived at the reception venue, where we were announced before entering to a standing ovation. Coreene's uncle Tim was the master of ceremony, he did a great job, he became famous in my family after that day.

On the top table was our parents on either side of Coreene and I. When it was time to eat, I was the only one not eating. I wouldn't be able to eat anything until after my speech because of my nerves. As we got to the desserts part of the meal, the speeches started and went on for a while, I was touched by a lot of what people had said. When it was time for my speech, I was nervous at first but became more comfortable as time went on. I really wanted to show God's hand in our journey to encourage people that didn't go to church why it's important and the benefit. We all had some laughs throughout and then I finished and at that point, I knew that I could fully relax as there was nothing left for me to do – what a day!

For the day, I had two organisers, my aunty Mia and aunty Amelia, they did a fantastic job and shielded me from things that would have otherwise stressed me out or ruined my mood. After the reception party, Coreene and I were dropped off by my friends Liam and his wife to the Malmasion hotel where we would spend the wedding night. I would wake up the next morning next to my wife for the first time. It was all new and exciting. It felt weird for me, all my life sex was wrong because I wasn't married, but now sex was good because I was married, there was no guilt or shame, just love and peace.

One thing that I would learn that took place on the wedding morning, was that in my mom's and her neighbour's garden, a massive 10 ft hole just appeared, investigations believed it was something to do with a coal mine. The day before, My mom's neighbours were in the garden, they were in their 70s, if that happened a day earlier, things could have been much worse. My mom had kept all this to herself on the day of the wedding. This hole would mean that my mom, brother and sister would have to pack a suitcase and leave, they were put up in hotels for months, before having to live in a house in West Bromwich before everything was sorted. They would be able to move back home for nine months in total.

On the morning after the wedding day, Coreene and I just chilled out and rested, before going shopping. We were going on our honeymoon to Fuerteventura in a few days, so we would get what we needed for that. Later that day, we went home for the first time as husband and wife, again, all this felt new and exciting. I had been living in the house by myself since June, but now we would be living together, no more of Coreene leaving at 10pm – life felt great.

When we went on our honeymoon, it was a great chance for us to relax and unwind, it was also a chance for us to get to know each other even more. They say that you don't really know each other until you live together and Coreene and I couldn't agree more. I think this where true love formed, where you see all of a person, not just part of a person when you go on dates, but everything. You see all the things you never noticed before and even the annoying little habits. But until you see all this and still say, "Yes, I still want you and choose you," then is it really love?

I always say to Coreene that I don't think she could be with another man because of who and how she is, likewise I don't think I could be with another woman because of who and how I am. I think Coreene and I are made for each other; she is the female expression of who I am and I am the male expression of who she is. We complement each other so well and fit together nicely.

Although Coreene got sick with a cold part way through, the honeymoon went well, we were growing together more and more. When we got back from the honeymoon, things in our lives would change as we adjusted to married life. This would be the first time in my life that I wouldn't be going to Hill Top every day, especially on Sunday after church, which was alien to me at first, as I never knew anything else. My relationship with my mom would change, because now I was married, before I would talk to my mom about everything, but now there was a partial barrier as I wanted to respect Coreene's privacy, it would be the same with my friends too – my wife had to come first and rightly so.

Coreene and I would learn to work together in house and run our house together, to be fair, we had already spoke about this and we both laid out our expectations and were happy to serve each other in different capacities. For me, one of the hardest things that I struggled with was communicating, especially when we never agreed on something. This was something that we spoke about and worked on.

"You can be in the right, but if you put your point across in the wrong way, you can put yourself in the wrong."

After our honeymoon in September, it was time to manifest our goals, one was four holidays within 18 months, so in November we went to New York, we were both excited about this. My dad lived in New York at the time and would be just minutes away from our hotel, so we said we would meet up at some point. The day before we fly out to New York, my dad called me and randomly tells me that he had a girlfriend, the reason he was telling me this was just in case we saw her. That really threw me and messed with my head. Before this, my dad and I were on good terms, but when I hear this, I felt angry. I didn't get why he told me the day before I flew out, which would obviously mess with my head, especially based on previous experiences. I wouldn't know at the time, but he also called my mom to tell her also. My mom and I wouldn't mention or discuss this until I came back from holiday. In my mind, they had been divorced for over 10 years, so why would my dad need to hide this? I wouldn't hear his reason for another four years based on a series of events that would take place in the family.

To me, it felt like, when my dad would come to the UK, he would use my mom's car, get picked up from the airport/train station by her, go to her house as though he still lived there, go to Hill Top like before the affair took place, but if he was open about having a girlfriend, the news could jeopardise all of this. Plus, apart from my mom and sister, no one else really knew anything apart from the facts that my parents are no longer together and my dad fathered another child. But if people knew he had a girlfriend and he was still popping up, taking my mom's car, going to Hill Top, especially when it was Christmas and he would spend it at Hill Top instead of with his own family, then people would have something to say, I know that I would! So to me, it felt like he hid the fact that he had girlfriend, because he wanted to have his cake and eat it, as and when he felt like it – but that's just how it came across to me… I could be wrong.

When Coreene and I get to New York, we arrive at the hotel late due to traffic. I arranged to meet my dad on the day we landed, unfortunately it would be much, much later. My dad told us to meet us at a restaurant, as we get out of the hotel, we use google maps to find the location. As we go up in the lift, in my head I'm wondering if it will just be my dad. The door opens and we walk in, as I see my dad at the table, he's not alone. Previously when something like this happened at Alexandra stadium and the athletic event, I walked off as I made it clear I wanted nothing to do with any of his girlfriends, it made me feel like I was cheating or disrespecting my mom, especially as she never chose the current situation.

This time, I had more maturity to handle the situation, notwithstanding, it would have been nice to be told that he wouldn't be alone and be asked if it was okay. In my mind, it was a chance for me to spend time with my dad and Coreene, not for me to get to know the latest girlfriend that probably won't be here in the next few months, which became the case.

I walk in and put a smile on my face and was on my best behaviour. Afterall, I had nothing against this woman, she hadn't done anything wrong. As far as she was concerned, my dad was divorced for over 10 years, but had a good relationship with his ex-wife and children.

The evening was nice, the place that my dad picked was spectacular, the view was amazing, it was a skyline view of New York and the Brooklyn bridge. We had originally planned to see my dad once or twice and spend the rest of the time alone, as this was our first real holiday together since getting married, but my dad had plans for the whole trip. My dad's heart was in the right place. I was excited to see my dad in his new home country and he was excited to see us and show us around. One thing about my dad is that he has always been a giver and loves to help people, just like his dad, I'm pretty similar. He took us to the best restaurants and spoiled us rotten and we were both grateful for the experience and gestures, but we wanted to spend some time alone. Plus, I remember being young before my dad was making crazy money and being on holiday in Florida with my parents and my aunty Abigail at the time; we didn't go to expensive restaurants, we just had basic things like pizza but the experience was awesome! So in my mind, I wanted to create the same thing with Coreene.

One of the evenings, we're out for a meal, as was the case for the whole holiday, my dad's girlfriend was there. It's hard to say something about a situation when someone has been nice to you and treated you so well in a specific way, it's like the money spent silences your feelings and if you say anything you're ungrateful, so you say nothing and remain uncomfortable. On this particular night, my dad' girlfriend casually mentions the time she came to the UK and met some of my dad's family. When I hear this, I want to explode. It felt like the time I found out that his family met my half sister and her mother long before any of us knew about the affair. It felt like history was repeating itself, but the expensive fancy restaurants and all the nice gestures silenced me, I couldn't say anything, how ungrateful would I be to say anything?

Overall, Coreene and I enjoyed New York, but I had a bit of a sour taste in my mouth after the whole 'girlfriend' thing.

When I get back home, my mom and I speak and acknowledge the night that my dad called us both, but we don't really talk about it; it kind of just got ignored. The next time my dad comes to the UK, it's business as usual as though the conversation never took place. It would be two years before I would tell my sister, it was like I was meant to keep silent on the fact that my dad had a girlfriend, otherwise I'm causing trouble in the family. But the time was coming where everything that was in darkness, would come into the light…

Chapter reflections

- *When you've had successes in life, who are some of the people that you were wish were still alive to share the moment with and why?*
- *What are some of the sacrifices/changes that you have made for your spouse/partner? How did it make you feel?*
- *Have you ever been in a situation where you felt like you should have spoken out, but you kept silent? Why didn't you speak up?*

Chapter 20
Happy Wife, Happy Life

After coming back from New York, I wanted to continue with our goals of four holidays in 18 months, but the next time I would ensure that Coreene and I could spend some quality time alone, after all, happy wife, happy life!

Because of the way our life was unfolding, getting married and buying a house, then two holidays back-to-back, it felt like people were watching us, some just to watch us and some watching in amazement. But to me, this how it should be, especially when God is leading you.

Work was still going great and I was hitting my targets and getting my commission, which was more than enough to support our goals. Shortly after we got back from New York, we booked our next holiday for June 2019 in Jamaica, the RIU in Negril. I hadn't been to Jamaica since I was 10 years old, this was a holiday that Coreene and I very much looked forward to.

When we were in New York, Coreene was excited about her new life and now that we were back and had just booked Jamaica, it was like a fairy tale. She would feel guilty about the things that we were doing, especially when other people weren't doing it. I would tell her that we shouldn't feel bad because of the favour and blessings in our life and that others could have the same through God.

As we entered into 2019, we both would change our cars. This was part of our goals once we got married after we were strict with our money. I still had my car that had a dent on the side, but now it was my season to change. Every time we did things, Coreene would always say, "People are going to think we're rich." To be fair, a lot of things were happening one after another, but what people won't know is that everything was planned years ago and we were patient. So that year, we both changed our cars which we were both excited about, especially me.

In 2019, I decided I wanted a new role with better prospects and benefits at BT. My role was desk based in the office, but I would started attending meetings face-to-face in London weekly, so that when I had an interview, I could demonstrate that I had already been doing the role.

I got an interview at BT for a role, the first interview went really well. I was given a brief and told to present a PowerPoint presentation for the second interview for the hiring manager and her manager. It felt like the job was in the bag, because of this, I felt like I didn't need God's help. At the interview, I do my presentation, as soon as the interview was over, without anyone telling me, I knew I messed up and that I had completely missed what they asked me to deliver. The interview was in Birmingham city, I remember sitting in New Street station really low, but humbled. I had got to a point where I was arrogant enough to think that I was somebody without God, this would be a lesson that I wouldn't need to learn twice. That year, I would take more interviews and be unsuccessful, I was desperate to leave my current role for a better one.

In June, Coreene and I would go on our third holiday to Jamaica, and it came at a great time. I was constantly looking for a new job, so this was a good chance to switch off. The last time I went to Jamaica 24 years ago, I stayed with family in the countryside and never loved it. But this time, we stayed in a hotel, all inclusive. We had an amazing time! The food, the restaurants, the beach, the night entertainment, jerk chicken and jerk pork on the beach, personal bar in our room – Jheeezz! Whilst we were out there, Coreene's aunty Ruby was there too with her husband and her friend and we all went to Rick's Café, which for me was an amazing experience, I never wanted to leave Jamaica and was determined to return very soon.

Around July that year, I get another interview for a better role, more money, more commission, company car and working from home – this was my dream job. At BT, there were different levels, there was SME level, which was local businesses like chip shops or hair salons, there was mid-market, where I was at the time, there was corporate, where I would be interviewing in June, then Major Corporate and finally Global. For the role in Corporate, I had gotten to the final stages, there were only three candidates and only one space. I had my final interview with the hiring manager and his manager. I was really nervous but the interview went great and I was really proud of my performance. This time, I was fully prayed and fasted up, I learned from my past mistakes. In the interview, there was a real-life scenario, where we had to come up with solutions. What I came up with was so good that the manager never thought of it, which lead to a mini meeting during my interview between both managers about why my idea was never thought of. When I left the interview, I was more than satisfied with how it went.

About a week later, I got a call to discuss their decision, I got lots of positive feedback, but they decided to go with another guy because he was already in a role that required the skills they were looking for, but I was at peace, because there was nothing else that I could have done. In my mind, as long as I have prayed, fated and given my all, there is nothing else that I can do and the role isn't for me.

Around September that year, I was selected for another interview, at this point because all other interviews had come to nothing, I was very blasé. This interview was much higher up in the Major Corporate division of BT, you wouldn't be wrong to say this was out of my league. I remember sitting in my car before the interview, not really caring after all the disappointment. I go to the interview and there's two people there, which is highly unusual for a BT first interview. Normally, you meet the hiring manager and then if you're successful, they arrange an interview with their manager as it needs two people to sign off on a new start. As the interview takes place, it was quite simple and I was able to answer the questions and give real life examples quite easily. A few days later, I get the call that I got the job, I couldn't believe it, I had jumped a whole level in BT and got promoted. After travelling from Willenhall all the way to Solihull, I would finally be able to work from home, with a better pay and a company car – Wow! I didn't realise how big the promotion was until months later when people would ask me how I moved from Mid-Market to Major Corporate, one manager even said, "Not to sound disrespectful James, but this is a major jump for you, I don't know what you did in your interview, but it worked,", other people were amazed at my promotion, but I just gave God thanks.

When I told Coreene and my family, they were over the moon and proud of me. This job would further help Coreene and I fulfil our goals. We were going from blessing to blessing and from strength to strength.

I started my new job in November of 2019, it was around this time that there were news reports of a disease in China called Coronavirus. But to me and most people, that was a China problem and nothing for me to worry about, or so I and everybody else thought.

As I was adjusting to my new job, we decided to book our 4th holiday to hit our personal goal. We booked to go to Majorca for five days, it was another chance to get away and spend time together. It was the first time either of us had ever been there. Although the weather wasn't blazing hot, it was still nice at times in terms of the heat. It was around this time that we booked to go back to Jamaica the next year in June, but this time with my family, it would be my first family holiday since around 2014 and I was really excited as I always had great times, plus it was a chance for Coreene to get to know my family better – so the adventure would keep going. I was keen to keep my new wife happy and spoil her.

In church, after Coreene and I got married, she left her church and joined me at New J. For about a year, neither of us would do much in terms of ministry and work in the church, it was just time for the both of us to settle into our marriage. It was around about this time that Coreene joined the worship team, in her old church, she was part of their worship team and would in this ministry at New J. My sister and her boyfriend Darrell were also on the team, so at least Coreene knew some people.

After I found out that my sister was dating, I was very, very, very, that's a lot of 'verys', but I was this keen to meet up with Darrell to understand what his intentions were for my sister. Since my dad left to live in another country, I always felt responsible for my brother and sister, especially as I was much older than them. I just wanted to take care of them both and make sure they had everything they needed. Before I got married, I had standing orders set up for both of them where I would give them monthly pocket money. I just wanted to do everything that I could.

Now that I learned that my sister was dating, I just wanted to protect her heart, especially after my experience with heart break years earlier. I contact Darrell and set up a day and time where we can meet and talk. We met at Starbucks at the Village hotel in Walsall. We spoke for a while and I asked all my questions, by the end of the conversation, I was a fan of Darrell and have been ever since. As time went on, I would watch him with my sister and how he was with my family and it felt like he was always there, he just fitted in and I felt relaxed that he would look after my sister.

When I got back from holiday, I was extremely focussed on work, then out of nowhere, my manager left to go to work for a competitor. This was shocking to me, as he would have known he was leaving when he was recruiting and hiring me, so why go through all of that if you were leaving? As we entered in December, my team was given a new manager. She was a lot nicer than my old manager and wasn't as demanding. We met up for a couple of times to officially meet and discuss my role and targets.

Around this time, there were rumours that BT were looking to make some changes, following the recent arrival of the company's new CEO and these changes would come in the form of job losses. In different sectors of BT, they were getting rid of some of the higher-up managers. Looking back, they were doing this in my old role in BT, but we were told there was nothing to worry about.

After attending my work's Christmas party in Birmingham, I broke up for the year. Coreene and I spent the Christmas period together and with family. There was one evening that we were meant to have my cousin Charlotte and her mom, my aunty Amelia round for the evening. Only Charlotte made it, as Amelia was not feeling to well and was tired, I didn't know but would soon find out that this was a serious illness.

As the new year started, there was more and more news about this disease called Coronavirus and how it was spreading, I think at this point there were cases in UK, but it wasn't anything major to worry about. Besides, every now and then, there's a new disease, this will come and go like all the others – or at least that's what I thought.

Work was going fine, in this role, sales were a slow burner, the main challenge was just getting time with prospects, so most of my time was spent trying to get in front of directors and CEOs of the organisations in my territory.

Amelia's sickness had got pretty serious at the start of 2020 and she had gone in for an operation. After the operation, things looked good and it seemed as if everything was fine. She was up and awake, speaking and laughing as per normal. Some point later that evening or overnight, she took a turn for the worse. Just like the case when Daddy Fletcher first got sick, my memory is pretty foggy around specific details and the exact orders of timelines, but after that day, Amelia wasn't conscious ever again. All the family and friends were at the hospital daily. At this point, no one knew what would happen next.

Chapter Reflections

- *What have been some of your goals that you have set for yourself in the last five years? Did you hit them, if not, why not?*
- *Have you ever had a phase in your life where everything you touch turns to gold? If so, explain.*
- *What were your thoughts of the Coronavirus back in late 2019?*

Chapter 21
Unprecedented Times

In early 2020, it fell like the end of the world was starting. This Coronavirus was starting to get more and more serious. My job at work was a field-based role where I was meant to go out and meet clients face-to-face, but a lot of businesses had stopped doing that as there was a lot of uncertainty. BT as a company had told us that we were not allowed to go out to meetings either. In the UK, there were more and more cases of people with this Coronavirus coming through, on the news they would give daily figures. Around this time, people were weary of going to church too, in fact there were people a church who had the disease and, in some cases, looked like they would never recover.

We were truly in unprecedented times; this was a phrase that was used over and over again. Zoom became a popular means of meeting people, with the phrase "you're on mute" getting repeated time and time again.

At Hill Top, we all stopped going so much, because elderly people were considered the most vulnerable, so we all wanted to protect Mommy Fletcher as much as possible.

At the hospital, Amelia was still unconscious and the doctors were doing everything they could. There was lots of family and friends there daily showing support. Again, I don't remember the timeline, but it came to a time where the doctor said there was nothing that they could do. My heart was broken, Amelia was still young. I had a lot of fond memories of Amelia, especially from my early years. She was a very generous person, who loved to help people in any way that she could. She was a gift to the world and anyone that had the pleasure of meeting her would agree.

My heart was broken, so I couldn't imagine how her husband, Geoff and her daughter, Charlotte felt. Amelia and Charlotte were best friends and did everything together. I'm very close with my mom, but I wouldn't disagree if people said that Charlotte and Amelia were closer. I hated situations like these, because there's nothing you can do and no amount of money or anything can help. I mean what do you say in a situation like this, especially as a Christian, were we are meant to bring hope to people? It felt like the foundation of my mind were slowly cracking, but again, if this is how I'm feeling, what about Charlotte?

Once we got the news that there was nothing that the doctors could do, they moved Amelia to a different ward with her own room, just like with Daddy Fletcher. My head was all over the place, at this stage in my life, my faith was pretty strong, so when Amelia first got sick, I and all the Christians in the family were praying and were confident of healing. But now things had escalated and she was put in a room to be made as comfortable as possible. With Daddy Fletcher passing, I could take that, he was old and had lived a full life and I get that no one will live forever. But with this situation, this was not the case and this is the thing I couldn't accept. I was praying to God begging Him to intervene, I was even doing what Jacob was doing when he was in a crisis where he said, "God if you help me, I promise to do 'X'. I'm sure everybody else had the same prayer."

I took time off work like everybody else and a rota was made to ensure someone was with Amelia 24 hours a day. It wasn't long before the call came in that Amelia had passed… why God? How could you let this happen? Why didn't you do anything? We prayed and we fasted! If she was older and lived her whole life, then yeah, I get it, but not like this! I was so angry and resentful towards God. Yes, I was a Christian, yes I was baptised, yes I knew the word, but that's just how I felt.

I arrive at the hospital and met the rest of the family, just like when Daddy Fletcher was there, I was useless and silent. At the time when Amelia passed away, Geoff was at a hospital in Dudley having his usual dialysis procedure. His daughter had to FaceTime him, as this was the only way he would be able to see Amelia and say goodbye.

Amelia passed away on the 19th of March and on the 16th of March, three days earlier, Boris Johnson announced the nation's first lockdown, so after this week, access into hospitals for guests and family would be stopped. These were truly unprecedented times!

After a while, we all leave the hospital, I was going to go home, get changed and then meet everyone back at Amelia's house. From the Queen Elizabeth hospital to my house is about 20–25 minutes. I didn't even reach home and I got a call from my dad. At this point, the tears that I had been shedding for Amelia on the drive back were beginning to stop. My dad then says that Geoff, Amelia's husband had just passed… I nearly crashed my car, the tears came back again, I had to pull the car over and just cry and cry. Geoff wasn't sick like that, he had been having dialysis for a while, this totally took me and everyone by surprise. It was like the world was just falling apart, all these deaths and a worldwide pandemic where you can only leave your home once, it was too much for me.

I regained my composure and get home, when I break the news to Coreene that both Amelia and Geoff had passed away, she falls backwards, before catching herself and hitting the floor. Because I had cried myself out when I pulled the car over, I thought I was okay. I sat down and put the TV on and went to Netflix, I mean, when two people in your family die at the same time and there's a national lockdown, what else is there to do? As I flick through options on Netflix, this massive wave of grief comes over me and I break down and cry like a baby all over again. All I kept thinking, was if I felt this way, imagine those who saw Amelia on a daily basis feel.

Around the time that Amelia passed, Grandad Beckford was sick at home, as it was lockdown, my aunty Paula had been staying with him to look after him. He got sick to the point where Paula had to call the ambulance. He was taken into hospital and I believe there were no visitors allowed at this time, it was just phone calls from the NHS staff to see how your loved ones were doing. Grandad was put on a ventilator, the hospital believed that he had Covid, although in the season, whenever anyone got sick or died people just seemed to record Covid as the cause.

My faith was already crippled after losing Amelia. I remember going for daily walks with my mom, brother and sister at this stage of the lockdown and my mom could see that I was struggling and this lockdown never helped. She said she was speaking to my dad when Grandad was admitted to hospital and she said people were praying for Grandad, to help inspire hope. My dad replied, "They also prayed for Amelia," and he was 100% right and I agreed with him at the time.

Grandad was still in hospital, it hadn't even been two weeks since Amelia passed away, when the family got the call that things weren't looking good for Grandad, I believe they let some people in to see him. Later that day, I was doing some work, my mom calls and says that Grandad has passed, I was so numb on the inside, it was like I had no feelings, all I could do was say, "Okay." I hung up the phone and kept working, If I kept working hard enough, I wouldn't have to deal with this pain, I could tell myself Grandad was at home fine, but I couldn't see him because of the lockdown. A few hours later, I had to face reality and started crying again, this was truly unprecedented times. This was too much for me.

The only silver lining in this, was that it brought me closer to my dad's side of the family. The family planned the funerals for Amelia and Grandad and they would take place one week after each other. Because of the lockdown and all the restrictions, there was no church service, it was just straight to the cemetery and you were only allowed 30 people in attendance and there were strict time limits for the length of the ceremony, but the family made the best out of a restricted situation.

To this day, it still doesn't feel real that they're not here, it's like they're away on holiday or something.

The worst thing about it was that after all that, people would have to pretty much face the next few months alone in their own homes because of the lockdown. I felt weird about leaving my house more than once, in case a neighbour reported me. There had been incidents were people were fined for breaking rules. I would go to my mom's house but wouldn't go inside, I'd just sat at the door, just in case. All church services around the country were online only, everybody had to adjust and do it quickly. This felt weird because you missed out on the atmosphere of being in church and not everyone, especially older people knew how to use technology to meet up virtually.

Things at work slowed right down, as many businesses closed down or began to struggle financially, this made it incredibly difficult to sell. BT were still making changes, at this stage, I was on my third manager in five months as they were still making redundancies and doing a lot of restructuring. The whole economy was suffering, with many people losing jobs and not knowing how they were going to pay their bills. Shortly after, the government introduced a furlough scheme where, if you qualified, you could receive around 80% of your salary. People were out stocking up on toilet paper till there was none left. I remember going shopping one time and you were only allowed a maximum of two of the same item. These were crazy times. Schools closed, so people had to work from home and home school their children. Many pupils who were meant to take exams were given scores based on their predicted grades, which in some case affected what university they could attend. Many people were now suffering more with mental health issues and domestic violence and divorce was on the rise. The football season was suspended for a while, leaving Liverpool fans wondering if they would get their hands on the Premier League trophy after all these years of trying… unprecedented times.

From March when Amelia passed until September, I wasn't doing well at all, I felt low constantly and because of lockdown, I was stuck in one place. I still hadn't gotten over what to me was an injustice, in terms of Amelia's untimely passing. With Grandad Beckford, that was easier to come to terms with because like Daddy Fletcher, he was older and had a full life in terms of years. During this time, I just stopped praying and reading. At night, Coreene would come to pray with me and I would say that I couldn't, so for a while, it was just her praying for me. I was getting frustrated because I wanted to get back up, but couldn't, plus I was looking for a 'word'/preaching that would give me the strength to get back to where I was.

Meanwhile at work, BT were still making changes by making people redundant. I got the news that I would have to interview for my job, or for another role within BT or risk having no job at all. At this point, I was numb that I didn't really care at first. I interviewed for my current role and at the same time I was looking for different roles too.

Around this time, I get a request to bring a word of encouragement and send it in, so that it could be used as part of the Sunday service. Because I had to do ministry, I had to fast and fix up. The message was called 'The Fight Back'. I sent it to my mom to look at, I wanted to make sure everything was Biblically sound. It was a message designed to encourage other people, but it actually encouraged me and gave me the strength to get up from my lowness. My mom had sent the recording to other people, and it helped others, then my aunty Paula started sending it out to people in the UK and overseas and they would send me people's responses, I wasn't the only one suffering during lockdown. I remember people asking Paula if there was a YouTube version, because at this time it was just a camera recording I did on my phone, shortly after, my dad would say that I should have a YouTube channel so people can access it more easily, so that's what I did and called it Blessed Central. I had this name from 2009 for a project that I had, but I never fully released or completed it. Blessed Central would become my only focus, it gave me an outlet and also helped me to work on my preaching and teaching. Not long after, I would start producing a message once a week, this was something that I never knew that I could do. Before, I would only speak maybe once a quarter, or being at New J, once a year, but as long as I was receiving a word, I would keep speaking. At the start, I would love doing it and became very passionate about it, but this would change as the weeks went on.

At BT, after interviewing for my role, I would find out that I was unsuccessful. Now that I was back to praying and fasting due to Blessed Central, I was praying for God to help me keep my job at BT. I found a few more roles that I was interested in and had some interviews. If I never got a job by 31st October, then I would have to leave BT, so I had around 6–8 weeks to make things happen. Because I was doing Blessed Central, that diverted my focus away from the risk of being unemployed.

I had the other BT interviews and was unsuccessful, so now I couldn't afford to put all my eggs in BT's basket, so I looked and got interviews for external companies, one of these companies was Zoopla, it was a three-part interview process, where I met their recruitment team in the first instance, followed by an interview with the manager Adam. Adam and I hit things off from the start and he was impressed with my CV and previous achievements. After meeting with Adam, the last stage involved a presentation to Adam and the Sales Director followed by questions. I left the interview feeling pleased, as I said everything that I wanted to. A few days later, I got the call saying that I was successful, this was literally days before my BT contact would be ending and where I would have been left unemployed, it was perfect timing and the first bit of good news I had in a long time.

During this time, I was still putting out content weekly for Blessed Central, but now I was having issues. I started struggling with my self-esteem, I felt that people were looking at me like, "Who does this guy think he is?" some people would make sarcastic comments about me being 'famous'. So each week, I literally would pray to God and say that I didn't want to do it anymore. Whenever I created content, after editing it and uploading it onto YouTube, the hardest thing for me to do, was to share it on WhatsApp, Facebook and Instagram. On top of that, when I first started, I would get a lot of good feedback, likes and views, but as time went on, they all dropped drastically. Apart from certain people in my family that would support and encourage me, I just felt alone and thought, *Why am I even bothering?* I wasn't just speaking and making videos, I was on another level in terms of my prayer and fasting and to be honest, after finishing work, all I wanted to do was have a beer and watch football as opposed to extra studying and fasting.

I remember one week, I saw someone post something on social media saying something like, some people only do things in church for fame. So immediately, I thought, *is he indirectly talking about me?* That night, I just laid on my sofa in a foetal position having a pity party, I was done, until Coreene spoke to me and helped me to regain focus as to why I was doing what I was doing and that comments from a few individuals out of seven billion people on the earth shouldn't bother me. It was conversation to slap me back in position.

Every time I wanted to quit, it was like God would send someone who listened to a message and it helped them, plus this was definite character development for me. By the time I did my last video in December that year, I learned to upload the video to social media and then switch it off, rather than judge myself by the amount of likes or views. I remember speaking with Bishop Brooks about it all and he said, even if it helps one person, then that's enough.

Another reason why I started doing Blessed Central, was because at that time in my life I was frustrated because I felt like I was wasting my gift in the church, people in my family and friends would ask me why I wasn't been used much at New J, which further added to my frustration. I felt like the guy in the parable with the talents that Jesus spoke about when he never used his talents but buried them instead. With Blessed Central, I could empty myself of everything that was in me, hence me releasing a video every week. In my head, I was thinking:

"If I die today, what am I leaving behind?"

This was part of my motivation.

At my job at Zoopla, I would spend the rest of 2020 in training, getting me ready to start selling in January, I joined at a good time. As we were approaching Christmas that year, the nation and the world were still in lockdown, the rules had fluctuated throughout the year in terms of meeting with people and how many people could gather together inside and outdoors. Boris Johnson would announce that for five days, families were allowed to gather, but no more than three households, or something like that. I think the government knew that most of the nation would just do whatever they wanted and no rules would stop families meeting up, especially after the year we had all had. As we entered into the new year, lockdown rules would resume and as we looked forward into this new year, there didn't seem to be any light at the end of the tunnel, everyone was desperate for a new season where we could all get back to some form of normality.

Chapter Reflections

- *What was your experience of the Coronavirus lockdowns?*
- *Did you find any silver linings during this time? If so, what were they?*

Chapter 22
New Seasons

As we entered into the new year of 2021, it wasn't until around March before things started to look like normal again, kids were back at school, pubs, restaurants, cinemas and sports events were getting ready to go back to a form of normal. Even at church, services were coming back around this time. The world was entering into a new season, a season everybody had been waiting for and welcomed gladly.

At church, I had joined a group called FutureSpark, this was created by Elder Karl, I was meant to have been involved from 2017, but because I was planning a wedding and looking for a house, I decided not to get involved at that stage. It was a group of brothers that were a similar age to me. Most of the guys had been in the group for a while and already had good relationships with each other, so I had some catching up to do. The year before, we all had a zoom meeting during lockdown, just to check in on each other make sure that everybody was okay.

Things at work were going well overall. As an Account Manager, we were targeted on upselling to our current clients as well as bring new clients on board. When I first started, I found upselling really easy, but I found new business a struggle, even when I hit my target, it came with a real fight. I decided to network with people from the team in order for me to get better. This really helped, I took bits from each person and made it into my own. By the time we got to June, I had mastered it and never looked back. I would go on to hit my revenue target and never miss, with my new business target, I missed once in February, but since then would go on to hit it 15 months in a row. The main thing I wanted was the '12 Months' certificate, that's where you hit both targets 12 months in a row, there was only one person out of 17 who had done this and I was keen to be the next. I got into a routine of praying and speaking declarations from a book called 'Prayer Rain', that specifically focused on hitting sales targets and to this day, it has helped me. I, by experience have seen the difference in my performance when I do and don't include God and put Him first.

> *"Seek the Kingdom of God above all else, and live righteously, and He will give you everything you need." Matthew 6:33*

Because of the impact of Covid, there were still restrictions on travel in most countries, so because we couldn't travel, the best thing was a BBQ in the summer. The year before we had some great times with multiple BBQs and this year would be no different. It was just nice having family around, playing music, with some food and drinks, I think the whole country were having BBQs during this period.

One of the last BBQs we had was in September, it was mainly for my sister as she just graduated, but it was also around the same time as my birthday. It was a nice evening and nice way to wrap up and finish the summer off.

After spending a bit more time with the guys from the FutureSpark group, I decided to invite them all round for an evening, so I could get to know people properly. Nicholas was the first to arrive, when he first came in, he was a bit sheepish. He said he got me an alcoholic drink but wasn't sure if he should bring it as a gift, apparently people thought I was this goody-too-shoes church boy that only read the Bible and was no fun. I quickly brought him up to speed and gladly accepted the drink.

As the rest of the guys arrived, we ordered some food and talked. The night was an outlet for some of the guys, it was a great evening, we laughed, some cried because of what they were going through and we prayed. We had some real good conversations to the point that I said, something like that night should have been recorded and shared to help people, because there's a lot of men out there that are struggling and have no one to speak to.

Elder Karl called a meeting with us all and gave us a project involving writing a book, where everyone would write one chapter each. We worked together to do our first draft, but at the same time, the idea of recording us having conversations like we did at my house was raised, so we ran with it. Nigel, one of the guys, knew a videographer and said that we could use his house to record, so we set the date to record for Saturday 27th November and in the meantime, we would work on Elder Karl's book project.

Because of the lockdown, there were a lot of things that had to be put on hold, one of those things were baby Christenings. During lockdown, there were a few babies born in the family, my sister-in-law had two more baby girls. Shabeena had her second son, John and in June of that same year, my cousin Rachel had her second child, Luke; Nina was her first, born just a year after Ethan.

The first christening after lockdown was for John on the 14th of November. It took place at my old church, after the main service. After this, everyone went back to Hill Top for food. Shabeena had gone all out in terms of decorations, there was even a curtain like material hung up as a background for pictures.

Although it was John's christening, all the pics were of and included Mommy Fletcher, everyone took pictures with her. It was strange that the evening happened like that. At that point, the family prayer meetings were still going, the theme was 'My Journey', where each person spoke about their life and all that God had done for them, firstly to remind themselves, but also to encourage everybody else. Mommy Fletcher was one of the last people on the list and she gave her life testimony and showed us her journey.

Later that month, on the 26th of November, in the early hours of the morning, I could hear a phone vibrating as Coreene and I were in bed asleep. I knew it wasn't a text, because it was a long vibration, at first I thought it was Coreene's phone, but it turns out it was my phone, I had a missed call from my mom. I already knew that a phone call at this time of the morning meant bad news.

I called my mom back, I hear the panic in her voice as she's trying to calm herself down and get her words out. She had received a call from Sally, she found Mommy Fletcher unconscious and had just called the ambulance, when I heard this, I was instantly fully awake. I told Coreene what I had just heard, I immediately get up and washed my face and brush my teeth as I wait for my mom to come from around the corner and pick me up. I remember brushing my teeth, I was talking to God, but not praying to Him, if that makes sense. I knew that Mommy Fletcher didn't want to be here anymore, ever since Daddy Fletcher passed, she was never the same and who could blame her after being married that long and losing your spouse. Even in her prayer meeting, she mentioned going to heaven where Daddy Fletcher is. As a family, we wanted Mommy Fletcher here for our benefit…

As my mom gets in the car, she's trying to get a hold of people who weren't answering, I just sit there in a daze, we had heard no update. The journey to Hill

Top is around 15 minutes, but this journey felt like an hour. As we pull up round the corner, there's a line of cars because the ambulance had blocked the street and no one can get past. I tell my mom to come out and I'll park round the corner. My mom leaves the car and runs inside. Once I park the car and run to the front door, I have no idea what to expect. I walk through the kitchen and see the paramedics filling out paperwork, in the living room, Mommy Fletcher's body is laying lifeless on the main sofa… tears start to come as the reality starts to settle in. I can't believe Mommy Fletcher is gone, I can't even say that I was heartbroken or crushed, I have no words to describe how much love I had for her and how much I miss her to this day…

This passing hit even harder because this meant everything would change at Hill Top in my mind and also, she was my last grandparent to go, this marked a new season that we were all entering into. As the morning went by, bit by bit all the family came, it reminded me of when Daddy Fletcher died and people came in at different time and were hit with reality when they see the body.

After the family organised the next steps, people went back home to change before returning later to see what they could do to help. By this time, Coreene was there, as we left and walked to the car, as soon as I got in, I broke down and cried from my soul loudly. Once we got home, I didn't want to sit there and do nothing, so I decided to go back to work, I needed something to do and think about.

The next day was the recording of the first episode for the FutureSpark podcast, I wanted to cancel because of how I was feeling, but because it had taken so long to organise, I decided to go ahead. I just felt like I was high most of the time, but it was a good distraction to have. We shot two episodes, the first was about marriage and the second one about low mental health. The point was for us to be as open and real as possible and take people through our journeys. It was a good day and I'm glad that we continued.

Meanwhile, at my old church, they too had been planning an event where they invited people to church for fellowship, but when Mommy Fletcher passed away, they too were stuck in terms of what to do, thankfully they also went ahead and it was a good time.

"Life doesn't stop, even when you're at rock bottom, sometimes you have to find strength to keep on going."

From the time Mommy Fletcher passed away, I felt different, I had the fire of passion to work and get things done, something that a lot of people would notice and tell me about. It was like a mantle had been passed down to the generations below, in the same way that money and possessions would be passed down. Either way, I would ride this wave and use it to my advantage.

As the year was closing out, the guys in FutureSpark and I would try to get our first draft done in time for Elder Karl's first deadline, but in the end we would miss this. We would have a call with Elder Karl to reset our focus and a new deadline was given for the new year.

The family were trying to organise everything for the funeral to see if it could be done before the new year, but after a while, it became apparent that this wouldn't be possible, so it would take place at the end of January. In the meantime, plans for the funeral would continue as we all prepared for our first Christmas without Mommy Fletcher. It was a tough time, but people handled it in the best way that they could.

During this time, my dad had flown over. Mommy Fletcher played a huge role in his life, so he wanted to be here. At the point when he arrived, there hadn't been a decision on a date for the funeral, so he would end up staying until after the funeral.

For me, Christmas felt weird, especially as Mommy Fletcher had only died a month prior. My mom had decided to invite everyone round to her house for Boxing Day, this used to be an annual thing for the family when I was younger, so it was nice to do it again and have the family around.

On the morning of Boxing Day, my mom texted me saying that Lilly, my half-sister is down. I knew that was code for "Lilly is down and will be here later with your dad for the family get together." Since the whole situation with New York, nothing was ever discussed, things went back to normal where my dad would come to the UK, use my mom's car, spend most of his time at my mom's and my mom would make dinner for him, almost like nothing had ever happened, which confused me emotionally and psychologically, especially now that you have girlfriends that come to the UK with you. But I held my peace. I have a massive rant and rave to Coreene, I didn't understand why my dad and Lilly would be at my mom's family Christmas event, surely my dad would spend time with his family and Lilly meet his family, rather than with my mom's family. After all, you chose to divorce my mom, so why then would you pick and choose times and events where it's convenient for you to be around. My emotions were all over the place, partly because I had a lot of things built up and had never been able to speak because it's never been a good time to talk and partly because I was still grieving.

I go the event later on with my best fake smile, but inside I'm fuming. I look at my mom and Calesha and they seem fine, just like they have always been in the past, so once again, there's something wrong with me and I'm the only one with a problem.

The evening was great and everyone had a great time with games and karaoke. I went to bed late that night but was up at the crack of dawn, I couldn't sleep, this whole thing was bothering me, but this time, I wouldn't ignore my feelings, I wanted to talk. I couldn't work out if my dad was using my mom and taking advantage of her by 'imposing his will' or if my mom was a willing participant.

I speak to my sister Calesha and much to my surprise, she felt the exact same way as me, so why weren't we all talking? I decide that I want to deal with everything now and have a meeting. I get to my mom's, my dad wasn't there but was expected anytime soon. So I ask my mom how she is and how she feels about the situation, because again, I don't know if she's a willing participant to what I see from the outside looking in.

"When you haven't identified why a person is in your life, you're not able to define the relationship and so there's no boundaries or rules of engagement. Define every relationship in your life!" Kevin Hutchinson.

This quote summoned up what I saw in my parents, people didn't know if they were together or not, there was no definition to their relationship and thus no boundaries in my opinion. My main thing was to protect my mom's heart. Women feel and react differently to men, they see things on a whole other level and I just wanted to make sure that my mom was okay.

My dad arrived part way through the conversation with my mom. I explained what was going on and said how I felt about this whole situation, including how I felt years prior in New York. I didn't mind my dad moving on and having girlfriends, but to me there was no difference now between their relationship at that point and when my dad first cheated. After I laid out why I believed this with clear examples, it became evident for others to see. I just said that the two of them should talk and have clear boundaries, so both people are emotionally protected and now that I had said my peace, that I wouldn't say anything else moving forward. I felt content and at peace now that I had got everything off my chest.

As we entered into the new year – 2022, Elder Karl had requested three goals that would push us (FutureSpark guys) and challenge us for the year. My three goals were to launch the FutureSpark podcast and social media, write a book and buy another property. But before I got involved in any of that, I wanted to focus on the funeral, I was down to give a speech. Originally, I think people wanted me to preach, but when the topic came up, it was only a few days after Mommy Fletcher passed and I was an emotional wreck, so agreed to do a speech instead. That's one of my life's biggest regrets, because I know Mommy Fletcher would have wanted me to do it and I felt like I let her down.

On the morning of the funeral, I felt okay at first. Everyone was meeting at Hill Top, where we would be picked up by the funeral cars. I was fine up until I got in the car and I started to feel very nervous, as soon as we got to the church at Gibson Road, I threw up, but it was just saliva as I hadn't eaten anything. I spent five minutes in the toilet regaining composure before coming out again.

The service was very nice and having a clip from Mommy Fletcher's 'My Journey' prayer meeting was a nice touch, something that a lot of people commented on, as many people hadn't seen that before. The family were very happy with the send-off.

When we got to the grave side, it was time to start digging, I did a share for some time and then got tired, then I had a tap on my shoulder, my brothers from FutureSpark were there and helped with the digging, I had other friends and family like Ashton, my cousin Llewelyn and Aiden there too, who also helped. It was nice to know that people had my back.

After the funeral, in my head I was questioning whether things in the family would be the same again. Hill Top had been the family hub all my life, people would visit Hill Top to see Mommy Fletcher and check on her, but what now? Thankfully, Sally let the family know that she didn't want anything to change and that Hill Top would be the same, which gave me and I'm sure others peace of mind.

After the funeral, the next few Sundays at church were difficult, it would be three weeks until I could stay in church when the worship team were singing without breaking down. Not long after that, one Sunday after church, my uncle

Mark came to me and asked, "Are you okay?" I responded, "Yes, I'm fine," as you do.

Then he looked at me in the eyes and asked again "Are you okay?" Before I could answer, he hugged me and tears started falling, then he said, "I love you." This broke me and started my tears off again. It was something that I needed but didn't know that I needed.

As we ended that month of January, the FutureSpark guys and I worked together and finished our first draft collectively and handed it in to Elder Karl. In February, I was down to preach, I was originally asked to do it the same weekend of Mommy Fletcher's funeral but thought it would have been too much for me. The title of the message was 'God Created…' based on Genesis 1:1 where God created the universe. I got some help from one of mentors Elder Keith from church, he gave me some great advice and challenged me with my approach. He was a seasoned preacher with decades of experience, so I was more than happy to absorb all his experiences and advice. It's funny, we met up the week before I preached, he asked me how I was and where my head was at, the last time we met, I felt frustrated because I wasn't doing much, but this time I was content speaking once or twice a year, now I had other things to occupy my time.

Up until this point, I had never done an altar call when I preached, I had always handed over to the service leader, partly because I never knew how to do one and also because of a fear of rejection. Imagine doing preaching for 20 to 30 minutes, you do an altar call and no one comes? But Elder Keith said that I must do one and he taught me how. When I preached, it was a different style to how I normally speak and I didn't know how it would come out, but God moved and when I did the altar call, the altar was full, God had showed up and the people responded.

Around this time, after everything that happened with the funeral and the fact that we couldn't travel for two years, I booked a trip to Jamaica with Coreene for the end of April. It was something to look forward to and not too far away. At the same time, my family were looking to go away the same year in August to Turkey, so we decided to join them as the last family holiday was cancelled due to Covid. So for now, it was all about the gym and getting 'beach' ready lol.

The guys and I launched the FutureSpark Facebook and Instagram page, to build awareness before we launched the first episode. We put up motivational and inspirational quotes, along with our profiles, so people knew a bit about us. The first episode would get released when I got back from Jamaica in May.

Around this time, I would reconnect with Aiden, we had a difference of opinion at the start of lockdown before Amelia passed away and never spoke for the two years. When we met up and talked things through, it was like we had always been speaking. We spoke on different occasions and caught each other up in terms of events that happened in our lives over past two years.

The year before, my mom had been put forward for the Bulter's Trust award, she had made it through the different stages and had finally been picked. It was an award that was issued in Oxford by Princess Anne, the family and I were so proud of her and her achievement. I was fortunate to have the opportunity to accompany her. It was the same day as my dad's birthday, 14th March. After speaking with my parents last year after Boxing Day, I felt the need to remove my dad from the Fletcher's family chat, not in a nasty way, but in a separation way. My mom wasn't in the Beckford's family chat, so why would my dad be in this one?

When we arrived in Oxford, my mom and I grabbed a quick bite to eat. I was taking lots of photos and taking in the scenery, it was beautiful. My mom was really modest, so people never knew she had this award, so I was more than happy to be her PR and Marketing manager that day. I let the world know and showed all the pictures and videos on Facebook, Instagram and WhatsApp. I was celebrating like I won something.

For the actual ceremony where Princess Anne would be, there was a rehearsal, people were taught how to address Princess Anne, what to say and what not to say and when to stand and sit, it was very interesting. At the reception/after bit, Princess Anne joined everyone and had conversations with people, she seemed very down to earth, she was very sharp and paid attention to detail. It was great to be there, it was something that I had never experienced before.

The next morning, I had made my decision about my dad, I removed him from the group and then called to explain why, from that day my relationship changed with my dad for the better! Now I speak to my dad more than ever and it's a relationship that we have, as opposed to being something that hinged of my mom being a middleman – I like it. Every son needs their father, no matter what the age.

That same month, I had a meeting with Elder Karl to review my goals, I had started everything with the FutureSpark podcast goal, now it was time to move onto the book. In my head, I was thinking about doing 10 chapters based on 1,500 words each, but Elder Karl was saying to double it, but that sounded a lot. I had never really written anything, let alone a whole book. At that time, I had zero words, but before I went to Jamaica at the end of April, I would have 28,000 words and had my first consultation with a book publishing company. The goal about property, would wait until the book was done or nearly complete.

In early April, my dad had planned to come to the UK because of work, I was actually meant to be in London that same week for my job, so we arranged to meet. Unfortunately, I got really sick around the time, so never made it London, then Coreene caught what I had and was also sick. In hindsight, we were both glad that we were sick at this point as opposed to the week that we would be flying out.

My dad planned another day to come up to the Midlands later that month, initially he would be meeting Calesha and Christian, I was still 'touch and go' with my sickness, so wasn't sure. My relationship with my dad was better now, he made me aware that he had a new girlfriend and that she would be coming. I respected and preferred that he was upfront with me, so didn't mind as much as I did in the past. But it still felt like I was cheating on my mom, but at the same time, we were in a new season, where everything was out in the open.

All five of us meet at a restaurant by Hill Top. I felt a bit awkward but tried to be as normal as possible. Amongst all the general chit chat, my dad was speaking to me about his job, we always asked how the other was doing in relation to targets. This time he mentions that they are looking for salespeople and he thought of me. The package was a much better package that I had with Zoopla, so I was more than open to the opportunity. Later that week, I would send him my CV and wait to hear back.

Overall, the day was fine, it never lasted long as Calesha, Christian and I had to go out and my dad had plans too.

As the holiday to Jamaica was fast approaching, all my focus and energy went into the writing this book. I would write after work till midnight sometimes and on weekends, I wanted to hit this goal.

Before going to Jamaica, I arranged a meeting with Nicholas from the FutureSpark group, he had been married for 16 years, had four daughters and multiple businesses, this as a guy I could learn from. I wanted to learn to be a better husband, I didn't want to think that because I earn decent money and provide financially that it meant that everything was great. Nicholas had spoken in one of the recordings of the podcast in the Marriage episode, which really hit me. He said he was working constantly to provide for his family and even got his wife an expensive gift and a luxury holiday, but his wife said she wasn't happy. He had been working so hard, that he was neglecting his family and this was something that I wanted to avoid. He asked about my daily timetable and how I spend my time, at this point, all my time was in the book. He looked at me and smiled and told me that I was being selfish, before going deeper, they call this a 'G-Check', when your friend tells you about yourself, in love, because they can see you messing up. It was a humbling experience. He told me not to get so caught up in the rat race of life to the point where Coreene feels neglected.

Originally, I was planning on working up until the day before the holiday and was going to take my laptop with me. He had to tell me four times not to take my laptop, I just didn't know how to relax and rest. I almost felt guilty if I wasn't doing something productive. He said to stop working from now and switch off now, so that when I'm on holiday, I will be present in the moment and not thinking about work or writing the book. It was the best advice I heard in a long time, and I was grateful that we met up.

Coreene and I went to Jamaica, and we loved every moment and every day of the holiday, it was our best holiday ever. The weather, the hotel, the food, the beach, the entertainment! Everything was great, I never wanted to leave, we were living our best lives as people kept telling us after seeing the daily pictures and videos. It was a great opportunity for Coreene and I to reconnect in a beautiful environment.

When we got back from Jamaica, everyone was talking and commenting on the holiday. At church, people were shocked that I could have fun, people still thought that I was this Christian robot, so it was good for people to see another side of me.

When I returned back to work from the holiday, I fell right back into the swing of things, I ended May hitting both my targets again for the 15th month in a row, it was amazing and I was proud of myself. We launched the first episode to the FutureSpark podcast, there were a few technical issues, but we were learning things as we moved forward, two weeks later, we released the second episode about mental health and stresses and pressures. Overall, it was a good first half to the year and I'm looking forward to the second half of the year and the second half of my life…

Chapter Reflections

- *Have you ever had a tragedy take place in your life, but you had to pull yourself together and complete a task/project? Reflect…*
- *What has tragedy shown you about yourself that you never knew before?*
- *What are your plans/goals for the next 12 months and five years?*

Chapter 23
Conclusions and Life Lessons

"Let us hear the conclusion of the whole matter…" Ecclesiastes 12:13 (KJV)

At the time that I have written this book, I am 36 years old. According the Bible, in Psalms 90:10, "The years of our life are seventy, or even by reason of strength eighty…" so I am halfway through my life or there abouts. After everything that I have experienced, I have certainly learned many life lessons and also come to some conclusions, that will undoubtedly help me to navigate through the second half of my life.

For me, the most important lesson is to put God first in life. As anyone can see from reading this book or looking at my life, God has been the biggest factor in my life. I couldn't imagine my life or even writing this book if I never knew God.

So many people only turn to God in emergencies or use Him as a last option. Some people only look to God solely because they don't want to die and go to hell, so He is just a passport to heaven. For me, I don't just need God in emergencies or for when I die one day; I need him every minute and every second of the day. This is more than a religion, based on what I can do or how good of a person that I am. It's about a relationship which grows and matures and ultimately helps me find my true identity – the person that I was originally created to be. There are so many people that are lost or uncomfortable with who they are, in most cases it's because they are currently someone who is living outside of their true identity, I'm just not talking about sexuality, race, gender etc… I'm talking about being alive! I'm talking about knowing that this is the person you are meant to be mentally, emotionally, psychologically, even down to the things that you produce in life. In today's society, there are too many 'Tarzans' out there – people living a life where they are trying to be something that they aren't or trying to fit in with everybody else in their environment.

The same way that Steve Jobs or Mark Zuckerberg created Apple and Facebook, is the same way that God created us. I believe if we are anything outside of what God created us to be, then we are malfunctioning and need help to come back into alignment. If your phone doesn't allow you to make phone calls, then it's not doing what it was created to do, it's malfunctioning. Who are you? Why are you alive today? What were you created to do? If you're stuck, go back to the creator and manufacturer…

"Before I formed you in the womb I knew you, before you were born I set you apart; I appointed you as a…" Jeremiah 1:5 (NIV)

A big part of our identity should come from our fathers, which leads to my next conclusion and life lesson. One of the biggest issues that I see in society, which has a huge knock-on effect is fatherlessness. This may be due to the fact that fathers are physically absent in the home, or they are in the physically and that's it. I think when we are children, even going up to adult hood, we expect our fathers to be perfect, with these expectations come huge disappointments. My relationship with my dad started out great when I was younger, we spent time together, I remember going to Kings Cinema in West Bromwich with my dad regularly and then going to McDonalds, just the two of us. Growing up, I would go football with him as he played Sunday league and I loved that. Then things would change as he came to watch me when I was playing Sunday league. There were many things that my dad taught me or things that he instilled in me from a young age, either directly himself, or through what his father taught him and I am hugely grateful for that as it's helped to make me the man I am today. I say all that to say, it's easy to forget all the good things that a person has done for you when they make a mistake – this was certainly the case for me. But as I have got older and matured, I have begun to learn that no one is perfect, including fathers. We expect perfection from them, when possibly they never got 5% of 'perfection' from their fathers and so on. Look for the good in people, especially fathers and no matter what, honour and never disrespect them. Speak to them about how you feel, address issues, but 'come correct'. This was definitely something that I had to learn.

My relationship with my dad isn't perfect, especially after everything we have been through, but it's so much better than where we were previously and this has come from us both making an effort and having open conversations. I love my dad and I am grateful that God gave me him as father and for all the positive things that he has deposited into me.

If you have an issue with your father, have you spoken to him about it? Have you given him the chance to explain his side? Have you taken time to understand who you father is – what is his relationship like with his father? How was his childhood? If you've tried everything, then forgive your father and tell him- it's not for him, it's for you! Let him know that you love and respect him and that you are open to talk, if and when he is ready. Sometimes in life, you can only control what you can control… but at least you tried!

One thing in life that many people are chasing for is love, particularly from a significant other. Searching for love and that 'special' someone comes with risks of heart break. One of the biggest lessons that I learned from my Pastor was:

"Ask question first, fall in love later."

This is one best bits of advice that I would give to anyone dating, especially if you're ready to get married. To many people get emotionally invested and 'fall in love' rather than 'walk in love' – remember, love is a decision, to make a decision without all the information or enough information is foolish.

If you're at the airport and you're flying to Canada and you meet someone who is flying to India, if you fall in love first before asking the right questions, the deal breakers, the non-negotiables, then after you fall in love you find out the destination, it puts you in an awkward position that could easily have been avoided.

Before you can ask the person where they're travelling to, you must first know where you are travelling to – which goes back to your identity. Knowing who you are and where you are going in life.

Understand the 80–20 rule, no one is perfect, realistically, you're not going to find someone that meets all of your requirements. So decide which aspects of non-negotiable and which ones you can be flexible. For example, for me, marrying a Christian woman was a non-negotiable, but even though I would have preferred a woman with no kids, this was something that I would have been flexible with, given the state of society and the majority of women in my age group. The problem some people have is that want it all! So as the Jamaican saying goes, "You pick, pick, pick, pick, until you pick... if you don't know, don't ask anybody lol."

Although I have only been married for a short while, the biggest conclusion that I have come to is, as long as I stay close to God and keep him at the centre of my marriage, the better husband that I am and the better the marriage is. Not to say you won't have difficult seasons, but God will be the rescue boat when the storms come into life and marriage, otherwise you can drown and divorce, or you remain together for show, but deep down you will be unhappy... but God!

All my life since the age of 14 when I heard that prophecy over my life, I've always been on the lookout for the fulfilment. I've found myself in life constantly chasing this, whenever an opportunity came along, I would ask myself if this is it? I heard the Bishop at my church say recently:

"Don't chase the promise, chase the God of the promise."

I've learned and come to the conclusion, that when something is meant and going to happen, then it will happen when it happens. I'm at a point now where I'm just living my life now and working on my character and refining certain things to be the best version of myself. When the time is right, thing will happen and manifest.

In the last few years, I have lost a lot of loved ones, whether is bereavement or a different form of loss which brings about personal loss; this is something that everyone must face. These were tough life lessons because these are situations that you have no control over. The only conclusion is that we can't control everything in life, but we can control how we respond. When you're at your lowest point, sometimes there are other people that are also there and they are looking to for strength and direction. So although you're at a low point, how you respond, doesn't just impact you – be careful, people are watching and need you to respond in the right way.

Conversely, when life is going great, don't forget God or the people around you that contributed to your success. There were many times in my life, where I desperately needed God and quickly forgot to pray, fast and acknowledge Him as I was when I needed him. I have learned that whatever it took to get you to point in life, is what will be needed to maintain you. Don't let success cloud your vision and effect your decisions.

As I look back over my life, it's not been perfect, but I am grateful to God for my life, my wife, my parents, my family, my church, my brothers and mentor in FutureSpark as well as my other mentors. As I look to the future, I more than ever can say that I can fly in my dreams, and I am very much looking forward to seeing how the rest of my life unfolds. Maybe in another 10 or 20 years, I will have the opportunity to write part two of my journey!

Thanks for taking the time to read about my journey. I hope I have encouraged, motivated and/or inspired you, so that you can not only fly in your dreams, but also make those dreams a reality!

Rosalynde Marsh is a writer whose associations with the medical profession as doctor and patient, as well as an advocate, have influenced her writing career. Her fascination with the community of a profession that is enshrouded in secrecy and inaccurate images has played a role in the creation of the characters in her writing, but the stories that she writes are not just about doctors and patients, but society at large, because in the end, that is what doctors are: a part of the wider community with the ability to change lives forever. Through the journeys of the characters, Rosalynde has always believed that a little part of everyone comes to life and explores life in a very different sort of world. Her writing is also influenced by literary friends across the world whose words have touched her.